REYNA ABURTO · TI
GANEL-LYN
ELAINE S. DALTON · LORI DENNING
KIMBERLY DOWDELL · JOHN HILTON III · DRU HUFFAKER
JULIE LEE · PORTIA LOUDER · BOYD MATHESON
WILLIAM PEREZ · MICHELLE PORCELLI
MARIANNA RICHARDSON · FIONA SMITH
CONNIE SOKOL · MICHELLE WILSON

IT WILL ALL BE *Worth It*

EDITED BY LIZ KAZANDZHY & KYLE LUND

CFI

An imprint of Cedar Fort, Inc.
Springville, Utah

© 2024 Cedar Fort, Inc.
All rights reserved.

No part of this book may be reproduced in any form whatsoever, whether by graphic, visual, electronic, film, microfilm, tape recording, or any other means, without prior written permission of the publisher, except in the case of brief passages embodied in critical reviews and articles.

This is not an official publication of The Church of Jesus Christ of Latter-day Saints. The opinions and views expressed herein belong solely to the author and do not necessarily represent the opinions or views of Cedar Fort, Inc. Permission for the use of sources, graphics, and photos is also solely the responsibility of the author.

Paperback ISBN 13: 978-1-4621-4759-5
eBook ISBN 13: 978-1-4621-4768-7

Published by CFI, an imprint of Cedar Fort, Inc.
2373 W. 700 S., Suite 100, Springville, UT 84663
Distributed by Cedar Fort, Inc., www.cedarfort.com

Library of Congress Cataloging Number: 2024934096

Cover design by Shawnda Craig
Cover design © 2024 Cedar Fort, Inc.

Printed in the United States of America

10 9 8 7 6 5 4 3 2 1

Printed on acid-free paper

IT WILL
ALL BE
Worth It

*To those who struggle, to those who doubt,
to those who are afraid, to those who are devout,*

*To those who believe, to those who don't know,
to those who belong, to those who feel alone.*

*He trusts you;
He believes in you;
He loves you.*

Contents

Introduction		1
I	His Hand Is Stretched Out Still	5
II	The Joy of the Saints	13
III	Discipleship Is Worth the Climb	25
IV	The Test	35
V	A Periwinkle Purse	45
VI	Finding Freedom in Prison	57
VII	The Three Goodbyes	65
VIII	The Race of Life	73
IX	He Meets Us Where We Are	79
X	Two Truths	87
XI	It Will All Be Worth It	99
XII	Divine Perspective	113
XIII	From Bad, to Worse, to Even Worse	125
XIV	Be Still, Together	135
XV	Healing the World One Heart at a Time	145
XVI	Are You Still All In?	157
XVII	Covenant Power	165
XVIII	The Price to Know Him	181
XIX	Fixing Our Focus on Jesus Christ	189
About the Authors		197
About the Editors		209

Introduction

By Liz Kazandzhy

"God never said it would be easy—He only said it would be worth it."

I've seen two camps of people when it comes to this quote. On one hand, there are those who embrace it, happily sharing these words online and displaying them on embroidered pillows in their living rooms. On the other hand, there are those who scoff at the fact that nowhere in recorded scripture did God (or the Savior) actually say those words. Personally, I find myself somewhere in the middle, recognizing the validity of the naysayers' claims but desperately wanting it to be true—hoping it will all be worth it.

Regardless of how you feel about the quote itself, there's something to be said about the sentiment of it: this idea that all the effort we put into living the gospel—sometimes at great sacrifice—will someday be rewarded. There's a hope simmering deep inside us that the soul-stretching challenges of mortality will not all be for nothing—that the price we pay for being "in the world" but not "of the world" will eventually be repaid in the next world. Surely, I'm not the only one who yearns for those blessings right now, hoping not just that my covenant keeping will be worth it in some future day but that it is worth it, right here and right now.

Thankfully—despite the fact that, as far as we know, the Lord has never literally uttered the words, "It will all be worth it," that's exactly the message He has shared with His people throughout the ages. And it's the message that's found within the pages of this book.

In the following chapters, you will read about those who have lost opportunities, those who have lost loved ones, and those who have lost hope. But you will also read about what they found: strength beyond their own, "rest unto [their] souls" (Matthew 11:29), and "peace . . . which passeth all understanding" (Philippians 4:7). Some experienced these sacred moments in sacred places, such as within the walls of the temple or while attending church. But others found the Lord outside of these dedicated buildings, like within the walls of a prison or while weeping on a bathroom floor. The words of each author are a testimony to the words of Sister Emily Belle Freeman, who said, "Jesus Christ will meet us *where* we are *as* we are."[1]

Beyond just sharing inspiring stories, the renowned authors who contributed to this volume have also shared timeless advice about how to make it through the "all" part in the phrase "it will all be worth it." By clinging to our covenants, selflessly serving others, patiently persevering, and fixing our focus on the Savior, we too can experience the comforting feeling that living the gospel really is "worth it," both now and in the future. For as the Lord Himself said, "He who doeth the works of righteousness shall receive his reward, even peace in this world, and eternal life in the world to come. I, the Lord, have spoken it" (Doctrine and Covenants 59:23–24).

If you have ever wondered if worthiness is worthwhile, if righteousness truly yields rewards, or if covenants are worth keeping, this book is for you. This book will buoy up your faith against the trials of today and days to come. Wherever you are on the spectrum of spirituality right now, our hope is that this book will strengthen your faith in Jesus Christ, who will give you refuge when you need it the most. In the words of the Prophet Joseph Smith, "Stand fast, ye Saints of God,

---

1. Emily Belle Freeman, "Walking in Covenant Relationship with Christ," *Liahona*, Nov. 2023; emphasis added.

hold on a little while longer, and the storm of life will be past, and you will be rewarded by that God whose servants you are."[2]

In closing, I'd like to share the words of President George Q. Cannon, an Apostle in the early days of the Church, whose testimony reflects my own:

> I know this is the Church and Kingdom of God. I know that those who cling to it will, in the name of the Lord Jesus Christ, receive glory and exaltation at his right hand. I know that people who love him, as the Latter-day Saints do, and are willing to make sacrifice, will not be forgotten by him. He will not forget them in the day that he makes up his jewels; he will bless them and honor them. That we may remain faithful and true unto the end, and be counted worthy to receive an exaltation in the kingdom of our God, is my prayer, in the name of Jesus Christ, Amen.[3]

Even back then, over a hundred years ago—and just as He has for thousands of years—the Lord was teaching the same message that He teaches through His prophets today:

It will all be worth it!

---

2. Joseph Smith, in *History of the Church*, 4:337.
3. George Q. Cannon, in *Journal of Discourses*, 23:133.

I
His Hand Is Stretched Out Still

By Julie Lee

I practiced how my baptism would go with my dad in our living room; he showed me just how to bend my knees so he could easily submerge me completely into the water without me losing my balance. I loved my dad. He loved Jesus, and He loved learning about His gospel. I still remember when he decided to read the Book of Mormon from start to finish in one day. He took a day off work, and with nothing but a tent, sleeping bag, and the Book of Mormon, he set out to complete the task.

That night he drove up the canyon, pitched his tent, and went to sleep. He woke up early the next morning and began to read. He read the entire book in one day, alone in his tent in the woods.

"Why?" people asked him. "Why would you do that?"

His response was always the same: he wanted to clearly understand the overall theme of the book. He thought reading it in such a short amount of time would help him do just that.

What did he find? With emotion in his voice, he told our family, "His hand is stretched out still."

I loved my dad for his devotion and study of Christ's gospel. I was proud to have him baptize me. He had taught me about Jesus, and I was excited to take this next step with him by my side.

As a squeaky-clean eight-year-old, I stepped out of the baptismal font feeling excited. It had all gone as everyone said it would . . . except for the Jesus thing. That part I hadn't anticipated.

"It was so cool!" I told my friends later. "I just had this really warm feeling and saw a picture of Jesus in my mind."

You see, when my face went into the water, I felt a warmth unlike the temperature of the font. In that moment of comfort and tightly shut eyes, I saw an image. Jesus Christ's face was in the upper right corner of my mind. His face was still and familiar; it came from a popular painting of the Savior—a painting that hung in my childhood home. The painting is called *Christ in the Red Robe* by Del Parson.

Something changed in me that day. And I was excited about it.

I would forever connect the face of God with warmth and excitement.

Because my father worked in the Christian art industry, I was exposed to different depictions of Jesus Christ from a young age. When I was around ten years old, I toured Derek Hegsted's studio inside of his home. Observing the artwork with my family, I paused at a painting of a little girl. She had blonde hair and blue eyes like me, and she was being held in the arms of the Savior.

Derek noticed me staring at the piece and spoke to me. "You know, you sure look a lot like that little girl in my painting." He reached into a nearby drawer and pulled out a 5x7 print of the image. He signed it and placed it in my hands.

I have since forgotten what he wrote, but I remember exactly how I felt. I felt warm and excited. Being the sixth of seven kids, I seemed to always be in search of something that set me apart from my siblings. What made me an individual?

When Derek Hegsted highlighted me as a lookalike for this girl in his painting, I couldn't help but wonder; did this mean I was famous? Did it mean I was pretty? Did it mean that Jesus loved me the way He loved the little girl in the painting?

In my mind, I answered yes to all three questions.

I went home that night and put the picture on my dresser so that I would be sure to see it every morning when I woke up. To this day, *I Will Not Fail Thee* is still my favorite painting of Derek Hegsted's pieces.

Depictions of Christ and His healing power would continue to play an exciting role in my life.

Seventeen years after this experience in Derek's studio, I found myself face down on the bathroom floor, my cheeks wet with tears of unanswered prayers.

I was twenty-six years old now. I was a wife. And I was a mama.

I had dealt with waves of anxiety and depression for four years. I had participated in different types of therapies. I had gotten on and off different types of medications. And I had seen many different types of therapists. I spent my free time scouring online lists of how to cure anxiety and depression.

Learn a musical instrument. I picked up the guitar. Check.

Exercise daily. I religiously made sure to get my workouts in. Check.

Meditate. My YouTube homepage was nothing but guided meditation videos. Check.

What about resources to help me access the love of Christ? How did I get that excited, warm feeling back? That feeling that reminded me that He loved me?

I attended the temple weekly. Check.

I read the scriptures and prayed multiple times a day. Check.

I taught my kids about a Jesus whose love is exciting, warm, and can heal anything. Check.

These resources and habits were helpful. They each served a purpose and helped me deal with this anxiety and depression that showed up with terrifying force in my twenties. But I didn't want these resources and habits to just help me stay afloat—not when I knew Deity was capable of making it all go away.

I saw Christ in my mind holding that little blonde-haired and blue-eyed girl from Hegsted's studio. I wanted to feel like that again. I wanted to experience the excitement and warmth that can come from feeling the reality of the Savior's love.

The bathroom was my safe place to fall apart. I had a toddler and a baby, and I was determined that they would never see me upset like this.

Today I had left the baby sitting safely in a bumbo on the floor of the living room, with my toddler sitting nearby next to a basket of toys. He loved to shake noisy playthings in front of his baby sister's face. His antics made her belly laugh, which made him laugh too.

Like so many days before, I locked myself in the bathroom, turned on the fan so my children couldn't hear me sobbing, and collapsed to the ground.

I prayed all the time. But today was different. Today I would be healed because today I would try something I'd never done before.

I lowered my body flat against the cold, dirty tile and stretched my arms across it so that my fingertips brushed the edge of the tub.

"Heavenly Father," I began, "I know that through Jesus Christ, anything is possible. You see, there's this story in the Bible where a woman has an issue of blood for twelve years, but through her faith, she touches the edge of the Savior's robe and she's healed."

I stretched my hands just a little further.

"I'm asking you—no, I'm *begging* you, God. I'm giving you everything—all the faith I have left. Please let Jesus appear before me right now. Please send Him. Please let me touch His robe and have Him heal me. I promise that if You do, I'll spend the rest of my life testifying of His healing power, and I'll be Your servant forever. Please, God, please. I've done everything. Please, I can't do this anymore."

I waited.

And I waited.

And I waited.

And He didn't come.

It hurt my feelings so much.

Was His hand stretched out still—for me?

Where was it?

Where was He?

After a few minutes of crying and accepting the reality that no Deity was coming to heal me, I peeled myself off the bathroom floor. My mind was immediately hit with an image from my childhood. It was the Savior's face, the same one I saw when I was submerged in the water at my baptism—the face of Jesus in Del Parson's *Christ in the Red Robe*.

There was no warm feeling or excitement. I felt defeated. I can't remember if I said it out loud or just thought it, but I remember I spoke to this face of Jesus that I saw in my mind. "Okay then," I said. "If you aren't going to heal me, I have to do this with You a hundred percent by my side. There's no other way. We have to do this together."

I went to check on my kids and forced myself to tickle their bellies and kiss their cheeks, choking back the tears of disappointment that my God had not come to me.

I continued to forage through online lists of how to cure anxiety and depression. Several of them listed writing in a journal as a way to find relief.

A few weeks later, I sat at my kitchen table writing in my journal. I was taking another moment to let the tears come as I wrote about the suffering I was experiencing. I covered my face with one hand and let my hair drape across the other side, providing a space for the tears to fall without my kids seeing.

After a little while, I heard my toddler squawking nonsense as he waddled into the room. Have you ever heard a toddler try to imitate a real conversation, but they only know a handful of actual words? *They* know what they're saying, but no one else does. It sort of resembles what I picture a drunk, slightly literate penguin would look and sound like.

My son continued his jabber as he tugged on my arm sleeve. When he didn't get a response, he got more direct: "Mom. Mom. Mom!" I was jarred from my thoughts. I quickly wiped the tears from my face and looked at my son. "Sorry, Sam. What is it, buddy?"

My boy, with blue eyes and blonde hair, looked up at me. And as clear as day, he excitedly said, "Mom. Jesus loves you!"

Then he turned with a graceless gait and waddled away.

I looked around. And then I looked up.

"Thank you," I whispered. "Thank you."

As one of billions of God's children, I felt seen. I felt special to someone—to Jesus. I felt a small level of excitement within me start to dance.

I sat at the table and thought about the way I held Sam up in front of the painting of Christ in our home. "Sam," I told him, "Jesus loves you." The painting was entitled *Seeking the One* by Liz Lemon Swindle. In my adult years, the painting claimed a space on the wall of my parents' home, and after my father gave it to me, it claimed a space in mine.

On the bathroom floor, I don't think I wanted a God as much as I wanted a magician. I wanted a transactional relationship, where if I asked for a blessing and pledged my allegiance, He would use His power to grant it. I felt deserving of it, I'd put in the work for it, and yet He hadn't taken away my anxiety and depression. I had seen His face when I stood, but I hadn't felt Him with me on the floor.

Sitting at the kitchen table, I received communication from God. He wasn't taking away my burden; what He was doing was reminding me that He was with me in bearing it.

His hand is stretched out still.

He'd shown me His love through the mouth of one humble enough to receive it: a child who couldn't formulate a coherent sentence to save his life.

A miracle like that? That felt exciting.

After my son left me at the table, these are the thoughts I felt:

"I see you sitting there at the kitchen table, trying to keep your pain private—trying to keep it from those you love. I see your effort. I see your discipline. I want you to know that I *was* there on the bathroom floor. Julie, I see you."

This moment was one of many when I felt Jesus with me as I learned how to grow through challenges. I began to believe, understand, and see what my friend and former seminary teacher David Wetzel taught me after losing his son to SIDS. He is possibly the most warm and excited person I've ever known, and he was so happy to tell me, "Julie, God isn't the *cause* of all things. He is the *context* of all things."

Do we believe in a magician or a God? Do we believe in a God that *micromanages* our mortal experiences? Or more often, do we see Him comfort and strength support us as we *navigate* our mortal experiences. Do we see Him saying "I see you" through tender mercies and tender people?

Are we excited about that?

As I look at the patterns of my life and look for Him, I see that Christ is more involved in my life than I ever thought possible—not as a magician, but as a God.

Around this same time of life, my father left organized religion and came to the conclusion that he no longer believed in Jesus as a figure of Deity.

This disclosure floored me.

I stared at *Seeking the One* by Liz Lemon Swindle, the piece he'd given me. Was there still healing from Jesus to be had? Could I still feel the warmth and excitement of His love that carried me through challenges in the past?

Was my Jesus a God I knew only through the teachings of my earthly parents, or was He a real being who could be deeply known by anyone who sought Him for long enough and hard enough?

I looked back at my life again. I read through my journals, searching for every spiritual experience I had recorded. I began compiling a document that I called "The Book of Julie." This would be my record of those warm, exciting feelings where I felt the love of the Son of God.

I saw the consistent patterns of His care in my own handwritten history. The evidence felt clear. Yes.

Yes, His love had carried me and would carry me. And yes, the excitement of His revolutionary love for all mankind was available and waiting for me to embrace.

His hand is stretched out still.

While I loved *Seeking the One*, I wanted a new painting of the Savior. A painting that *I* chose for my own home. I knew Jesus now. I knew what His love felt like. I didn't need someone else to be my connection to Him anymore.

I had felt the warmth and excitement of Christ's love.

Now I wanted to find a picture that looked like it.

Jesus wasn't the cause of everything bad in my life; Jesus was the context of everything good in my life. Where would I find a picture of that? What painting looked like the Jesus I'd come to feel?

I am happy to say that after years of looking, I finally found Him.

It was a portrait of Christ based on a photo taken by an artist named Adora. A woman named Jenny Fowler received the photo and created a beautiful drawing of it.

What struck me most about this adaptation of Christ was His eyes. They looked the way He felt to me. When I met Jenny Fowler to buy the portrait, I mentioned Christ's eyes to her. "I see shapes in the reflection of His eyes," I told her. "He's seeing something in this moment. Can you tell me what it is that He sees?" She graciously told me she couldn't; she felt it was too sacred.

I don't know what Jenny Fowler meant to depict in the reflection of Christ's eyes. But I see a very vivid picture, and I can tell you that the scene I see testifies of His love and redeeming power to heal all pain in this mortal experience even if we have to wait until eternity for that healing to come.

His eyes are warm and what they speak is exciting.

His hand is stretched out still.

For three years now, Jenny Fowler's portrait of Christ has been claiming the best space on my wall. My home has changed three times since then. The painting hung in the house I left when my marriage ended. It hung in the basement apartment where I received the news that my sister died. Now it hangs in my new house, and while I'm not a kid anymore, I love to see His face every morning when I wake up.

Few days go by without me pointing to Jesus on the wall and reminding my kids warmly, "Jesus loves you."

My devotion to Him is *worth it*.

Why?

Because even though my life isn't perfect and hard times still come and to, I've seen what Christ's love can surpass.

I've seen what Christ's love can heal.

I've seen what Christ's love can help me create.

And that helps me to feel excited.

II
The Joy of the Saints

By Reyna I. Aburto

"No thanks!" This was my answer every time my aunt or one of my cousins would invite me to visit The Church of Jesus Christ of Latter-day Saints. I had been raised in the Catholic faith and would attend their services occasionally, but living a religious life was not a priority for me. I believed in God, I knew about Jesus Christ and His teachings, but I did not know Them well enough to be willing to get closer to Them.

I was twenty-six years old, living in San Francisco, California, after moving there five years before. I was married at the time, had a three-year-old son, and was busy trying to provide for him. My then husband had fallen so deep into alcoholism and drug addiction that he had stopped working. After years of trying to help him get out of that trap, I realized I had to protect myself and my son from the devastating effects of his addictions. I then made the decision to get a divorce. Even though I felt relief after taking that difficult step, I was deeply concerned about my son's upbringing and future. It was then, in the middle of all this turmoil, uncertainty, and fear, that a miracle happened.

I was living with my mother. On a Saturday morning, she felt prompted to visit her sister, who lived a few blocks away and had been a member of the Church for some time. During my mother's visit, a missionary couple came to see my aunt. They were pleased to talk to my mother and invited her to come to church the next day. When I came home from work that evening, my mother related how delightful her conversation with the missionaries had been and asked me if I wanted to go with her to their religious services the next day. This time I said yes. Now it was different—I had hit rock bottom, and even though I hadn't realized it, I was longing for something strong to hold on to. My willingness to soften my heart was the beginning of a new life for me.

I didn't know it at the time, but all those invitations to "come and see" (John 1:9) were coming from my Savior Jesus Christ through His followers. He wanted me to "partake of his salvation" (Omni 1:26) because "he inviteth . . . all to come unto him and partake of his goodness; and he denieth none that come unto him, black and white, bond and free, male and female; and he remembereth the heathen; and all are alike unto God, both Jew and Gentile" (2 Nephi 26:33).

As I stepped into the church meetinghouse that crisp October morning, I felt something I hadn't felt before. That's when I first experienced "the joy of the saints" (Enos 1:3). It was a stake conference in San Bruno, California, and the building was full of people greeting each other. From their bright countenances, I could tell how happy they were to be there. There was something in them that I couldn't put into words. Then the meeting started, and people of different ages and from different backgrounds spoke from their heart. Their messages were personal, powerful, and profound. They told stories I could relate to, and they testified of both simple and big miracles from Jesus Christ in their lives. I turned to my son seated next to me, looked up toward the ceiling, and offered a brief heartfelt prayer of gratitude to my Father in Heaven. I had found a safe place, a place where I wanted to raise my boy, a place that felt like home. I had found a place where I could possibly feel joy.

I made the baptismal covenant three weeks after and started on my journey as a disciple of Jesus Christ, where I have continually felt surrounded by His love through His Saints. Little by little, in small and big ways, I have experienced the joy of being part of a community of people who are sincerely trying to follow Jesus Christ despite the burdens that each of us may be carrying. For me, finding my Savior and getting to know Him in a more personal way has been a precious gift. It has empowered me to become who I am today, and His redeeming Atonement encourages me to continue becoming who I can be in the eternities.

I often think about what I felt that Sunday when I attended church for the first time. Why did I feel such a strong sense of peace and belonging? Why did I have the desire to stay and learn more? I believe that one of the factors that had the biggest impact on me that day was the people who were physically present in that meetinghouse—from the stake president to the stake and ward leaders, from the families to the individuals, including the children. Each person brought the power and the light that they had been endowed with as a result of their covenants with Heavenly Father, their faith in Jesus Christ, their knowledge of His restored gospel, and their desire and efforts to stay on the covenant path.

I feel that the beautiful, dedicated buildings play an important role in what we feel when we gather in them, but it is the people who make the greatest difference. The Spirit we feel in an empty building is not the same as when that building is full of Saints feeling joy together regardless of the hardships or the difficult circumstances in their lives. The that joy each of us brings when we gather is the perfect invitation for the Holy Ghost come and for God's purposes to be realized. Even better, we can feel and take that joy everywhere we go as we interact with others in the different spheres in which we find ourselves, most importantly in our homes and with our loved ones.

I could not be the same person after that day. The Spirit had made a lasting and undeniable impression in the "fleshy tables of [my] heart" (2 Corinthians 3:3). I had "come to myself," like the prodigal son. I had finally realized that I had been meagerly filling my belly with husks, perishing in hunger, and dressed in spiritual rags. I now had the opportunity to feast on the Bread of Life and the Living Water that Jesus Christ embodies and offers liberally. I was now merry and glad, wearing the protective robes given to me by my Father (See Luke 15:11–32).

Through the years, I have learned how important it is for each disciple of Christ to proclaim the "good tidings of great joy, which shall be to all people" (Luke 2:10). We are the means through which God brings about His work and through which the earth is being prepared for the Second Coming of Jesus Christ. You may be thinking, "You have an interesting story, but you don't understand. My story is different." You're right. Each of us has a different story, and we've all had different faith journeys. However, there is joy in walking our journeys together and in seeing beyond our mortal limitations and struggles to embrace each other as sisters and brothers who are children of God.

I have asked my husband Carlos and my friend Larkin to write part of their faith journey with the intention of showing how unique and special each person is and how each of us can partake of the Savior's goodness and salvation in our own way.

Carlos's Journey

Carlos' faith journey started in Mexico when he was a child. He shared the following with me.

> I remember the feeling of warmth I had inside every time I saw the missionaries walking on the street. In my ten-year-old mind, I wanted them to come to my house and become our friends. One day it happened, and they were sitting in our living room teaching my whole family.
>
> My mother, four of my siblings, and I were baptized and started attending church. My father was never baptized, but he was never opposed to us joining the Church. My older siblings attended youth activities during the week, and each time they came back, they were happy and would relate to my mother what they did, the games they participated in, and how kind the leaders were to them.
>
> Eventually, my mother was given callings in the church. She worked long hours sewing dresses to sell them to help provide in our home. When I look back now, I realize that she suffered from social anxiety and that it was difficult for her to perform well with others. I believe that this was a major factor in what led to us taking a step back from regular church

attendance despite the efforts of many members to help us come back.

Even though we did not attend church, we always felt respect for it and knew in our heart that its teachings, based on the gospel of Jesus Christ, were correct and true. However, as a family we succumbed to the customs of the world and, among other things, didn't keep the Word of Wisdom. I grew up without the protection that the gospel of Jesus Christ provides.

At age 23, I moved to San Francisco, California, to live with my brother who had been there for a few years. He would attend church occasionally, and I wouldn't go with him despite the fact that Elder and Sister Bangerter, a missionary couple, had been visiting my brother and me. When I was 27, I broke up with a girl I was dating and felt devastated. The weeks after were extremely difficult, and I was in desperate need of help and comfort. In the middle of all that pain, as I was driving one day, I stopped at a restaurant to use their public phone. I called my then ex-girlfriend, but she didn't answer. As I hung up, I felt the same discouragement and sorrow that had been overwhelming me for days.

Suddenly, still inside the telephone booth, I was overcome by some force that shook me and made me grab the phone again. Inside my head, I had a distinct thought: "Call the missionaries." At that moment of desperation, I knew they could be a source of solace, so I called them. They invited me to their apartment where Elder Bangerter gave me a blessing of comfort. Having been baptized through God's authority, I knew that the Church was the ideal place to find refuge from my anguish.

In the apartment I shared with my brother, we always had a copy of the Book of Mormon. During that time of deep soul-searching, I decided to open it and started reading it like someone who grabs a glass of water with an unquenchable thirst. I had two jobs at that time and not a lot of free time, and I would anxiously wait for the next chance to continue reading it.

It's hard to express with words the feelings I experienced and the impact that reading the Book of Mormon had on me. It was as if every word on its pages fell in fertile soil that was eager to receive a seed to start growing fruit. At the same time, the words of the ancient prophets were like daggers in my heart that caused a pain I knew was necessary to receive spiritual healing. Their testimonies of Jesus Christ were an invitation to turn to Him and to follow Him. They felt like buckets of water falling on the burning logs of my sins and suffocating the anguish they had caused for so long.

Soon after, I started attending church. The simplicity of the talks and the lessons had a similar effect on me as reading the Book of Mormon. I eventually received callings and was endowed in the temple. I can honestly say that the reason why I came back to church was because the teachings of the restored gospel of Jesus Christ were engraved in my mind, in my heart, and in every fiber of my being. And when I felt a pressing need for divine comfort and aid, something was awakened inside me. That feeling was combined with the understanding that we are our own agents and that we need to decide what to do with the things that are manifested unto us. I cannot deny that during the first weeks after I came back to church, the Lord comforted me through people who were making an effort to follow Him. He has done this to me over the years, and it has been clear to me that His Church is the place I need to be, regardless of what happens.

For me, the Church is everything. Because of it, I have what I have, and I am who I am. To be constantly exposed to the restored gospel of Jesus Christ makes me turn my mind and heart to Him and His teachings. The Church is like a filter through which I can go to clean myself from the impurities that surround me. To partake of the sacrament every Sabbath is the filter that I have available to renew myself. I also feel that it's important not to lose a sense of wonder for the simplicity and magnificence of this ordinance, through which the Lord extends His arms of love to us.

Besides the communion with God that I find in the Church, I feel that the sociability that I can have with my travel companions in this mortal journey is also important. I constantly learn from them, and hopefully they learn from me as well. Our life is constantly changing, and our personal circumstances regarding our health, employment, housing, marital status, and so on can change at any moment. It would be difficult to face these changes without the support network I have in the Church through leaders and members who try to keep their covenants.

I feel that the Church of Jesus Christ is a universal wildcard that adapts itself to our financial, cultural, social, professional, and intellectual circumstances and helps us be wiser in the way we live and relate with others. Even though it may be difficult for some, for me it is worth the effort to persevere and try to continue forging a relationship with Heavenly Father and Jesus Christ. That's because if we do so, when hard times come into our lives, They will manifest their love to us, either directly or indirectly through those who make an effort to follow Them.

At the same time, I feel that it's crucial that we have living prophets in our day. It's hard for me to imagine my life without being constantly exposed to the teachings, the guidance, and the counsel of men who have been properly ordained to be special witnesses of Jesus Christ. My trust and faith in them are immovable because they will never say or do anything contrary to our spiritual wellness.

Larkin's Journey

The following is my friend Larkin's faith journey, also told in her own words.

My faith journey has been a wild ride, with all sorts of twists and turns. I was raised in a faithful Latter-day Saint family. Seven kids in the heart of Utah Valley—it couldn't have been more typical. When I was about sixteen, a series of really difficult events led me to wonder if any of the things I had been told growing up were true. I lost myself in a storm of pain and confusion and no longer understood how I fit into my current environment. I felt broken—too broken for this Church—so I left in search of healing and answers.

After eight years of pain and wandering, exploring all sorts of different healing modalities and spiritual perspectives, I found myself living in Thailand, more lost than I was when I first embarked on my faith journey. I had tried everything to fill the void I felt inside and tried to put my broken heart back together. My whole life had become focused on healing, endlessly reaching for this elusive state of peace that so many therapeutic modalities and faith practices promised me, until one day I think I just became too tired to keep wandering. At the time, I was studying Eastern philosophy and religion as well as multiple different healing modalities. It was always one after the other, waiting to land on "The One" that would finally heal this brokenness I felt inside.

We were in the midst of the COVID pandemic, I was far away from my family, and my relationship with the man I thought would be my life partner was falling apart. Something was beginning to shift inside of me. Perhaps the terror of the current world events was shaking me up inside. Or maybe it was the sudden feeling of intense loneliness I felt as I was going through a challenging breakup, wishing I had loved ones nearby. All I knew was that something was not right. I was being kept up at night with this nagging feeling that there was something I was not seeing—another way. The reality that the world is in desperate need of healing was staring at me—and I think all of us—right in the eyes. But I kept thinking how the whole world does not have the luxury to travel to an island in Thailand and give all of their time and energy to healing themselves. And apparently, as I was beginning to realize, even *that* didn't seem to be enough.

I finally fell to my knees one night and prayed out to a God I was not entirely sure I believed in. I poured out my heart and soul that night. Calling out to Jesus, desperate for help and answers and willing to throw everything I thought I knew out the window to find it, I found peace that night—the peace I had searched for day and night for years. I realized that He was the answer to my brokenness, the relief to my pain that I thought I would never find. That was the beginning of the forging—or rather reforging—of our relationship. I soon learned how deeply I needed Him, and that as long as I remained close to Him, He would take me where I needed to go.

A few months later I was back home in the United States and found myself unexpectedly walking through the doors of a Latter-day Saint meetinghouse. He guided me here. I never would have thought I would be here. I was incredibly cautious and apprehensive about coming back to church. But something happened once I finally did—something I did not entirely understand at the time. After partaking of the sacrament, something shifted inside of me. It was subtle, but it was there. I felt the power of His holy priesthood working in me, cleansing me, healing me. And something inside of me knew that I needed this.

As I kept showing up, week after week, I learned the meaning of entering into a covenant relationship with the Lord. After so many years of being alone, the invitation to be more deeply bound to Him spoke to the deepest parts of my soul. I yearned for more of Him. Something in me knew that there was so much more available in our relationship, and I didn't want to miss any of it. I was experiencing the power that taking the sacrament every week brought into my life. The weeks that I missed it, I felt different—less connected and more susceptible to the pulls of the world.

After careful thought, prayer, and preparation, I made the decision to go through the temple and receive my endowment. What I experienced afterward further solidified my already growing testimony in His restored Church and the power of covenants. My ability to feel the power and presence of the Lord in my life expanded. It felt like more of Him—and more of myself—was made accessible to me. There are so many wonderful things that being a member of The Church of Jesus

Christ of Latter-day Saints brings into my life. It is strengthening to have a faith community. It allows me the opportunity to meet my edge and grow as a human being.

I find so much peace in reading the words of the Book of Mormon along with the other holy scriptures made available to us. Every time I attend the temple, I grow closer to the Lord and receive clarity to the questions in my heart. I could go on about the things I love about this Church. But what brings me back over and over, more than anything else, is the power and peace that having a covenant relationship with Jesus Christ brings into my life. This decision to say "yes" to a deeper relationship with the Lord and continue forward on the covenant path has made all of the difference in my life. And only this Church can offer me that.

I love Jesus Christ, and I love anything and anyone who brings me closer to Him. I know that it's not always easy. This journey has tried and tested me. But ultimately, I am better because of it. I know that this is the Lord's restored gospel where we can find truth and healing. I know because I have experienced it.

* * *

Carlos, Larkin, and I have experienced the joy of the Saints in different ways. Our stories interconnect because we have been a source of comfort to each other, and we have invited each other to come to Christ. For example, the missionary couple that helped Carlos come back to Church was the same couple that invited my mother to partake of the Lord's goodness, and Elder Bangerter was the one who baptized me. Carlos and I also happened to be in the same congregation when Larkin attended church for the first time in years. Her faith, the light that she emanated, and her eagerness to find solace in the Church of Jesus Christ drew us to her and allowed us to feel joy with her.

Each of us are constantly looking for and finding reasons to feel a sense of wonder toward the gospel of Jesus Christ as well as reasons to continue on the covenant path, bound to the Savior, allowing Him to guide us through His Spirit. He has given us this beautiful assurance:

Come unto me, all ye that labour and are heavy laden, and I will give you rest. Take my yoke upon you, and learn of me; for I am meek and lowly in heart: and ye shall find rest unto your souls. For my yoke is easy, and my burden is light (Matthew 11:28–30).

I was recently vacuuming the carpet in our chapel on a Saturday morning when the memories of my first experience at church came rushing to my mind. I was overwhelmed with gratitude for everyone who contributed to the presence of the Spirit in such a palpable way that day. I thought about the faithful members who offered their tithing for that meetinghouse to be built and maintained. I thought about those who cleaned the building and set up the chairs and the flowers before that stake conference. I thought about the stake leaders who prayerfully planned that meeting and the members who dutifully prepared inspired messages and sang sacred tunes. I also thought about each one of the attendees who brought a measure of the Holy Ghost with them. Without fully knowing it, each of them became an instrument in the hands of God for me to feel His love in a profound way.

That Saturday, as I was helping prepare the chapel for the Sabbath, I thought, "I wonder if tomorrow someone will come here for the first time and be able to feel the joy of the Saints as I did. I wonder if they'll ever know how much love and faith is put into preparing ourselves and our dedicated settings for everyone to feel the love of God, the enabling power of the Atonement of Jesus Christ, and the renewing influence of the Holy Ghost. I wonder if I will be sensitive enough to perceive their need for a warm welcoming."

One insight I have received from the parable of the prodigal son is that even though the father loved his son profoundly, he waited for him to come back home. He did not go to the place where his son was. He patiently waited until his beloved son came to himself, arose, and returned home. He waited, with a heart full of love and compassion toward his son, and when he saw him from afar, he ran, fell on his neck, and kissed him. Our Father in Heaven also waits for us by the road, patiently waiting for us to come to ourselves and to turn to Him. Every time that happens, He feels merry and glad—He rejoices together with His Son and His Saints—because one has been found after being lost (see Luke 15:11–32).

At times, I ask myself, "Where would I be if I had not accepted that invitation to come and partake of Jesus Christ's salvation? What would have happened to me and my son? Where would I have found the peace and solace I feel every time I partake of the sacrament to renew my covenants with Heavenly Father and to make a new covenant with Him? Where would I feel the joy of the Saints with people who are striving to be faithful disciples of Christ?"

On that same note, where would Carlos and Larkin be? And where would you be? More importantly, I ask myself, "What am I doing to welcome others as they come into a community of Saints eager to feel God's love and grace? What am I doing to give back to others the warm embrace I received when I came for the first time? How can I help others feel 'the joy of the Saints'?"

My invitation to you is the same invitation extended by the ancient prophet Omni: "And now, my beloved brethren [and sisters], I would that ye should come unto Christ, who is the Holy One of Israel, and partake of his salvation, and the power of his redemption. Yea, come unto him, and offer your whole souls as an offering unto him, and continue in fasting and praying, and endure to the end; and as the Lord liveth ye will be saved" (Omni 1:26).

We all take different paths in life because we make different choices and have different circumstances. But no matter where we are, what we have passed through, how lost we might feel that we are, the Lord Jesus Christ is waiting for us, to receive us, to welcome us. Only He has the ability to take everything that we've gone through and make it all worth it.

III
Discipleship Is Worth the Climb

By Michelle Craig

In a world that is becoming increasingly dark, divided, and demanding, I find great comfort and peace when I remember that we are beloved sons and daughters of God; that because of Jesus Christ's life and perfect loves, I can repent, I can change, I can feel peace and joy, and I can have the companionship of the Holy Ghost everyday. Because of the grace of Jesus Christ, I can do hard things. What a gift.

My brother Rob served a mission in Switzerland. At the conclusion of his mission, my parents picked him up and took our younger brother, Paul, with them. While serving, Rob grew close to a member of the Church who was an expert hiker. This man offered to guide them on a mountain hike—something my brothers had always wanted to do.

When the day of the climb arrived, my dad and brothers set off with their guide on their grand adventure. The first several hours of hiking were lovely—complete with scenic views and the sound of cow bells in the distance. I imagine they probably snacked on crusty bread and delicious Swiss cheese.

As they arrived at a small hut on the side of the mountain, the guide informed them that this was where they would spend the night. The real hike would begin in the morning. My dad looked beyond the hut and could see a large, rugged mountain peak looming in the distance. This was their destination. Dad spent the night restless, and it wasn't an uncomfortable mattress that kept him awake; it was the thought of climbing a mountain too steep and too rugged. He did not feel up to the task. During that sleepless night of worry, my father determined that he would simply go back down the mountain by himself and then meet up with his sons and the guide after they completed the climb.

In the morning light, Dad shared his plan with the others. In response, the guide simply asked, "Which of your sons are you going to take with you? The rule of the mountain is you never hike alone. You will need to take one of your boys back down with you." As my dad looked at my brothers' crestfallen faces, he couldn't disappoint them. He decided to try.

The expert—the one who had traveled that very path many times before—then gave my dad some excellent advice. His words in that moment gave him courage: "Put your feet exactly where I put mine, and don't look down."

In life, we want to be good; we want to find our individual errands from the Lord and somehow make a difference. But the truth is, there are times that the path looks too steep, and we feel unequal to the task that looms before us. We are afraid and wonder if the climb is worth the effort. But we follow the One who has gone before, and we try our imperfect best to put our feet where He has put His and follow in His footsteps. Love the Father, and love others. We look forward with faith, not down or back on mistakes, doubts, or fears. As President Jeffrey R. Holland taught:

> The past is to be learned from but not lived in. We look back to claim the embers from glowing experiences but not the ashes. And when we have learned what we need to learn and have brought with us the best that we have experienced, then we look ahead, we remember that *faith is always pointed*

toward the future. Faith always has to do with blessings and truths and events that will *yet* be efficacious in our lives.[4]

I had an experience many years ago that I have gone back to often when I feel inadequate, discouraged, and wonder if my efforts and offerings matter.

My children were young, and my husband was in school, working full time, and serving in a busy church calling. I felt I was running on empty keeping things going at home. I was happy he was having opportunities for spiritual growth, but meanwhile I felt I was stalled.

One night as I slipped into bed, I remembered I had not read my scriptures, something I wanted to do every day—but frankly, I didn't feel like it. I was tired and feeling a little sorry for myself. Feeling guilty, I opened my scriptures and told myself that reading just one verse would be fine and would meet my goal of reading my scriptures each day.

I opened my scriptures to a verse that has since become one of my very favorites, Doctrine and Covenants 64:33: "Wherefore, be not weary in well doing, for ye are laying the foundation of a great work. And out of small things proceedeth that which is great."

I will never forget the feeling I had. As I read and reread that verse, my heart was softened. The Spirit whispered to me that the "great work" the Lord spoke of could be my life—it could be my family—if I continued doing the small things that in the end would make a big difference, even if I did feel weary at times.

I put that scripture on my refrigerator where I saw it many times a day. It served as a visual reminder to keep doing those small, simple things that were of most importance with my little family and in my personal worship and development. They were and sometimes still are small things that weren't seen or recognized by anyone outside of our home: conversations in the car, preparing endless meals, packing lunches, waiting up to hug a teenager when they come home, making cookies, welcoming friends, reading scripture, and saying prayers. But God sees our efforts, and it is the small and simple things that make

---

4. Jeffrey R. Holland, "The Best Is Yet to Be," *Ensign*, Jan. 2010, 24; emphasis in original.

a lasting difference, not only in our lives but in the lives of those we love.

These things we do while climbing the path of discipleship don't have to be big and flashy things; most often, they will be small things. In the words of Mother Teresa, "Not all of us can do great things, but we can do small things with great love."[5] These small things done with great love are what it means to be a disciple of Jesus Christ. "By this shall all men know that ye are my disciples, if ye have love one to another" (John 13:35). Even in our weakness, this is a path available to all disciples.

I have loved acting on President Russell N. Nelson's invitation to increase our understanding of Jesus Christ by studying His names. "Study everything Jesus Christ *is* by prayerfully and vigorously seeking to understand what each of His various titles and names means *personally* for you."[6]

Two of my favorite names of Jesus Christ are both found in the book of Hebrews: "high priest of good things to come" and "author and finisher of our faith."

These are names that reassure my sometimes fearful heart that everything is going to be okay (better than okay) if I keep my faith centered on Jesus Christ—and not on my desired outcomes.

Sometimes I like to look at the 1828 Webster's dictionary when I'm studying. (It's the dictionary that Joseph Smith would have used.) I did that while studying these two names of the Savior, and now I love them even more.

Author means one who produces, creates, or brings into being.

Finisher means one who finishes; one who completely performs; one who completes or perfects.

Looking at Jesus Christ in this way helps me in the here and now as I walk the path of a disciple. I have hope, and I know all things can work together for my good as He "creates in me a [new] heart" (Palms

---

5. Mother Teresa, "Not All of Us," Goodreads, accessed Jan. 20, 2024, https://www.goodreads.com/quotes/6946-not-all-of-us-can-do-great-things-but-we.

6. Russell M. Nelson, "Prophets, Leadership, and Divine Law," Worldwide Devotional for Young Adults, Jan. 8, 2017, Gospel Library App; emphasis in original.

51:10) and as He perfects my faith while I offer up my imperfect offerings and two mites.

I know this about Him. I know that I am a beloved daughter of God, that His character is good and perfect as is His plan for each of us. His perfect plan is made possible by, and centers in, His perfect Son, Jesus Christ. It is a plan that honors agency. It allows each of us the opportunity to have a physical body and learn through experience what it means to walk in faith. Faith wouldn't really be faith at all if life were easy, if answers came quickly and easily, or if everything we prayed for was answered in the way and in the time frame *we* wanted. Tested, tried, and proven faith is the faith of a disciple climbing mountains.

Sometimes that faith is tested when we feel our prayers are not being heard.

I don't think I'm alone in feeling that there are times my prayers just don't make it past my ceiling or the roof of my car. The heavens seem silent. At times, I realize this is my fault. But at other times, this perceived barrier is there not because of apathy, laziness, or lack of effort on my part. Deep inside I know that my prayers really are being heard; I'm either just not hearing the answers or I need to be at peace waiting upon the Lord and trusting His timing.

When we find ourselves in this situation, and I think we all do from time to time, we can't stop keeping our covenants or stop praying.

There is nothing wrong with praying and asking for answers to our questions. In fact, we are commanded to ask, to seek, and to knock. I have found in my own life that some of the greatest growth comes during these periods when I feel like my prayers are going unanswered. It is during these times when we are literally brought to our knees that we find ourselves reaching out, pleading again, and again, and again. We hope and we rely on what we know of the character of God. He is good, and He wants to give us those experiences that will be for our best good. We trust that our loving Father in Heaven wants what is best for us. I find comfort in the teaching of Elder Richard G. Scott: "Our Father will always answer your prayers in the way and in the time that will be for your best eternal good."[7]

---

7. Richard G. Scott, "Using the Supernal Gift of Prayer," *Ensign*, May 2007, 11.

We are used to things coming fast, whether it's an Amazon delivery or an answer on Google. But God doesn't work that way. Things of most worth often take the most effort. Here's another comforting teaching from Elder Richard G. Scott: "His answers will seldom come while you are on your knees. . . . Be thankful that sometimes God lets us struggle for a long time before that answer comes. It allows us the opportunity to move forward with faith and do the best we can with what we have already received."

Each of us have opportunities to exercise faith, to show our wholehearted love and devotion to Jesus Christ and Heavenly Father in the small and simple acts of everyday living.

I am inspired by Ruth, a woman whose story is recorded in scripture. Her example of faith and love has blessed and strengthened countless individuals over the centuries. Hers is an example of devotion to her mother-in-law, Naomi, and to her God that manifests itself in small and simple ways within a family setting.

Ruth's story shows us how God is faithful to us when we are faithful to Him. Hers is not a story of comfort and ease; rather, it's a story of moving forward in the face of adversity and uphill climbs.

The book opens hard. Naomi, Ruth's mother-in-law, is an Israelite living outside of her homeland. Both her sons marry Moabite women, and a famine ravages the land. She experiences great loss—her home, her husband, and both of her sons. Despairing, Naomi releases her two daughters-in-law, now widows, to return to their families. She decides to return to Bethlehem, the land of her family.

One of the daughters-in-law, Orpah, accepts her invitation. The other, Ruth, responds unexpectedly, "Entreat me not to leave thee, or to return from following after thee: for whither thou goest, I will go; and where thou lodgest, I will lodge: thy people shall be my people, and thy God my God" (Ruth 1:16).

Ruth not only chooses to stay close to a widow who has lost everything; she also chooses to leave the land of her family. She chooses to abide in her covenants and in her deeply rooted love of God. Ruth loves God with her whole heart, and that love propels her forward, inspiring her to extend that love to others.

Sometimes when I read those verses, I like to imagine myself saying the following words, not to Naomi but to Jesus Christ: "I will follow you. Wherever you go, I will go. Wherever you stay, I will stay. Your people are my people. No matter what happens, I'm yours. I'm all in."

Ruth's wholehearted connection to others and to God through her covenants inspires me. How many years did it take until she experiences her happy ending with Boaz? We just don't know. But this we do know: that as we tether our hearts to God and to our covenants, everything is going to work out. The endings of our stories will be so much better than we ever imagined.

There is another woman in scripture I love. We don't know her name, but we do know she was a poor widow. Although her resources are limited, she is wholehearted in her faith and in her devotion. She is unnoticed by most, but not by Jesus Christ, the Savior of the world:

> And Jesus sat over against the treasury and beheld how the people cast money into the treasury: and many that were rich cast in much.
>
> And there came a certain poor widow, and she threw in two mites, which make a farthing.
>
> And he called unto him his disciples, and saith unto them, Verily I say unto you, That this poor widow hath cast more in, than all they which have cast into the treasury:
>
> For all they did cast in of their abundance; but she of her want did cast in all that she had, even all her living. (Mark 12:41–44)

Elder Dieter F. Uchtdorf taught:

> With this simple observation, the Savior taught us how offerings are measured in his kingdom—and it's quite different from the way we usually measure things. To the Lord, the value of the donation was measured not by the effect it had on the treasury but by the effect it had on the heart of the donor.
>
> In praising this faithful widow, the Savior gave us a standard to measure our discipleship in all of its many expressions. Jesus taught that our offering may be large or it may be small, but either way, it must be our *heartfelt all*.[8]

Her offering was small and simple, but it was also great.

In Mark 14:3–8, we learn of another wholehearted offering.

---

8. Dieter F. Uchtdorf, "Our Heartfelt All," *Liahona*, May 2022, 122.

> And being in Bethany in the house of Simon the leper, as he sat at meat, there came a woman having an alabaster box of ointment of spikenard very precious; and she brake the box, and poured it on his head.
>
> And there were some that had indignation within themselves, and said, Why was this waste of the ointment made?
>
> For it might have been sold for more than three hundred pence, and have been given to the poor. And they murmured against her.
>
> And Jesus said, Let her alone; why trouble ye her? she hath wrought a good work on me.
>
> For ye have the poor with you always, and whensoever ye will ye may do them good: but me ye have not always.
>
> She hath done what she could.

This offering was great—both in intent and in worldly value. Spikenard was rare and valuable in Israel. If Judas was right, the cost of this offering was the equivalent of a year's salary, or tens of thousands of dollars by today's standards. But the monetary value is not what matters to Jesus.

"She hath done what she could." She was wholehearted.

An alabaster box of spikenard. Two mites. Was one offering better than the other?

We often worry about whether we have done enough. Perhaps we compare our two-mite offering to the alabaster box and spikenard that our neighbor or brother offers. It just doesn't compare. It's not as big and certainly not as pretty. But we do not worship a God who compares the size or scope of offerings. If we have made and kept covenants, if we have "done what we could" with our time, our talents, our capacity, it is enough, and it is beautiful. The fact that we have given our "heartfelt all" is what will transform us and help us to become who and what the Lord desires.

The seventh verse in the beloved hymn "How Firm A Foundation" beautifully expresses my feelings:

> The soul that on Jesus hath leaned for repose
> I will not, I cannot, desert to his foes;
> That soul, though all hell should endeavor to shake, . . .

I'll never, no never, no never forsake!⁹

The last time I stood at the pulpit in the Conference Center in October 2022, I wanted to convey the feelings that had been pressing on my heart: feelings that we need to fight against apathy and be "all in" with the gospel of Jesus Christ, feelings that we need to act in faith and trust in God and in His timing. What I said then is my closing encouragement to you:

> My fellow disciples of Jesus Christ, with all my heart, I choose to stand with the Lord. I choose to stand with His chosen servants—President Russell M. Nelson and his fellow Apostles—for they speak for Him and are the stewards of the ordinances and covenants that tie me to the Savior.
>
> When I stumble, I will keep getting up, relying on the grace and enabling power of Jesus Christ. I will stay in my covenant with Him and work through my questions by study of God's word, by faith, and with the help of the Holy Ghost, whose guidance I trust. I will seek His Spirit every day by doing the small and simple things.
>
> This is my path of discipleship.
>
> And until the day that the everyday wounds of mortality are healed, I will wait upon the Lord and trust Him—His timing, His wisdom, His plan.
>
> Arm in arm with you, I want to stand with Him forever. Wholehearted. Knowing that when we love Jesus Christ with all our hearts, He gives us all in return.

Wholeheartedly following Jesus Christ is not a guarantee that life will be free of trials and difficult terrain. Difficulties and questions allow us to demonstrate our faith in, and love for the Savior. He understands. He loves and appreciates our imperfect efforts to do good and be good. And He is so anxious to bless us with every good thing. These good things are coming for each one of us who continues the climb, one foot after another. It will be glorious.

---

9. "How Firm a Foundation," *Hymns*, The Church of Jesus Christ of Latter-day Saints, Salt Lake City, UT, no. 85, Gospel Library App.

IV
The Test

By Lori L. Denning

Just recently, I was on a plane traveling for work. It was late and the cabin was dark. I had my phone out and was watching a movie. I sat in my cramped plane seat, and I was crying.

I like to think that I'm not much of a crier. I don't weep at the drop of a hat, but there are a few things that get me. I turned my head toward the window so my fellow passenger wouldn't see me, but there was no hiding it. I sat there, watching a movie I had seen a hundred times before, sobbing.

The young man in the seat next to me asked, "Are you okay?"

There was no denying my tears. "Yeah, it's just that I'm a sucker for a turnaround—a love story redemption."

"Oh," he said with a nod. "Are you watching a romantic comedy?"

"Uh, no," I said a bit abashedly. I turned my screen so he could see it: *Star Wars: Episode VI - Return of the Jedi* as Darth Vader, unmasked, lies on the floor in the arms of his son, Luke.

He paused, his eyes flicking back and forth from my tear-stained face to the screen to see if I was kidding. Then he nodded. "Yeah, that gets me too."

Darth Vader lies dying on the floor of the Death Star. His fierce mechanical mask is cracked, and his true face is revealed. His artificial suit is shattered, his body broken, and he is fighting for his last breath. Above him, his son, Luke Skywalker, who fought with love to save and redeem him. After saving Luke from the force lightning of Emperor Palpatine and sacrificing himself to save his son, Vader's last wish is to look at his son, not as Vader, but as Anakin Skywalker. Gone is his artificial mask and veiled eyes. Face to face, a son redeems a father, and the father has saved the son.

In a line packed with more truth than most for a science fiction space opera, Anakin speaks of the kernel of goodness that only Luke sees in him and says, "You were right about me. Tell your sister you were right." And then Anakin dies.

That is the part that gets me. Even now, retelling the story, my eyes mist over and my voice catches in my throat. While Star Wars is a movie, it tells the truth of redemption that I believe in deeply. It tells the story of a test—the trials, the challenges, and the temptations that all of us will go through in life. And it also tells the story of hope, hope that even the worst of us can change, that we can pass the test, and with the love of another, we can become something better.

Our lives are hard. We all go through many trials and tests. It's no surprise to anybody who's alive that life is full of challenges. We are challenged physically, mentally, emotionally, and spiritually. We will have family challenges, financial challenges, work and school and church challenges.

There are bright moments of wonder and beauty, and perhaps because they are not the norm, they stand out. But that wonder and beauty doesn't remove the struggles or hardships. On the other hand, those struggles and hardships are planned and part of what make the beauty and wonder so special.

I like to compare the scriptures with Star Wars, and while Star Wars may not seem like it has a lot in common with scripture, Star Wars highlights an event that happens in all of out lives. Scripture calls it The Test. However, scripture does an even better job in helping us understand The Test through the lives of ancient people who lived through challenges just like ours. Learning to recognize these pivotal moments in scripture helps us to recognize, navigate, and overcome them in our lives.

A Beginning

The concept of The Test isn't new; it's been there from the start. In the beginning, at the Grand Council in Heaven, the scriptures record a profound conversation between the Father and the Son, setting the stage for our mortal journey. They said, "And we will prove them herewith, to see if they will do all things whatsoever the Lord their God shall command them" (Abraham 3:25). It's clear, right from the first chapter of our collective story, that life is a test. The Test is a foundational part of the plan. It is baked into the very reason we're here. We are going to be "proven" to see if we will follow the Lord's commands.

The scriptures help us see that tests are a part of life, especially in the stories of the people we read about. The patriarchs, the prophets, the kings, and the disciples all face their own moments of testing. Many of these events are not random hardships; they're intentional moments crafted by God to see if His people will live up to the life He's called them to. These tests ask a very significant question: Will they act with faith, or will they lean on their own understanding and miss the mark? This isn't just a literary device; it's a reflection of a deeper truth that our lives are full of moments when we're asked to show where our loyalties lie—with God through our faithfulness to Him or with ourselves as we follow our own ways that often lead to disobedience.

The Test

In the Old Testament, the word in Hebrew is *nasah*. It occurs as a recurring thread, a scriptural motif that repeats, so we can learn from it each time it appears. The word means "test" but not like an exam or a simple, mundane pass-or-fail assessment. That kind of event is a *bacan*. A *nasah* is more than a momentary *bacan*. While translators often use the same word for either one, saying "test" or "trial," a *nasah* is bigger and more significant. A *nasah* tests something to see what it is made of. It reveals one's true character, who they really are.

There are myriad examples of The Test in scripture. It seems like the scriptures are a virtual list of people going through trials and tests.

It is Abraham on Moriah, grappling with the command to sacrifice Isaac, his son, his future, and the covenant promises. It is Moses at Sinai, where a nation's covenant with the Divine hinged not just on words spoken but on hearts changed. It is David facing Goliath, not just a giant of flesh and bone but a towering edifice of doubt and fear that besieged the armies of Israel. It is found in the stories of Hannah's silent prayers, Esther's courageous advocacy, Ruth's steadfast loyalty, and Job's enduring faith. This Test is vivid in the narrative of Nephi, who faces the daunting task of obtaining the plates from Laban, and in Sariah navigating the complexities of her family and the promises given to her. It echoes in the wrestling prayers of Enos, the leadership of Mosiah, the teachings of Alma, and the perseverance of Mormon and Moroni.

In our dispensation, it is in the unwavering strength of Mother Smith, in the steadfast devotion of Emma Smith, in the resilience of Hyrum, and in the steadfast actions and love of Joseph for the Lord. Each story and each character contributed to the ongoing narrative of The Test, an enduring testament to faith, endurance, and the transformative power of divine challenges. Through each trial, The Test is not just a moment of decision; it is a revelation of character and a defining point in the journey of faith.

The Test is a motif that starts at the very beginning.

The Test at Sinai

An example of The Test is the story of the Israelites at Mount Sinai. Just a brief journey away from the chains of Egypt, the children of Israel faced a divine test, not of strength or intellect but of faith and obedience. Here, amidst the thundering echoes of a past drenched in hardship and the anticipated promise of a land flowing with milk and honey, God laid before them a challenge as formidable as the mountain itself.

The air itself seems charged with the weight of the moment as Moses ascends, disappearing into the thick cloud where the voice of the Lord awaits. The Lord's voice that had shattered the chains of Pharaoh now it offers the children of Israel a covenant—a path to becoming a holy nation, a kingdom of priests. But the offer comes with a condition: "if ye will obey my voice indeed, and keep my covenant" (Exodus 19:5).

The response of the people is immediate—a resounding commitment echoes against the mountain walls: "All that the Lord hath spoken we will do" (Exodus 19:8). It is a pledge of allegiance, a vow to walk in the ways of the Lord.

This was the test of Sinai—not a momentary trial but the beginning of a lifelong journey of faithfulness. It was a test not just of the moment but of the heart, a question that would follow them through desert and valley, through battle and peace. Would they hold fast to the words spoken amidst smoke and fire, or would they falter, turning to the comfort of golden idols and the familiar path of doubt?

The narrative takes a breath and pauses at the cusp of a covenant. "If ye will obey my voice indeed, and keep my covenant," the Lord promises, "then ye shall be a peculiar treasure unto me above all people" (Exodus 19:5). For them, it is a future full of purpose and promise; Israel is to be a kingdom of priests, a holy nation set apart.

With Moses as their intermediary, the people are instructed to prepare themselves, to consecrate themselves for the day when the covenant would be sealed. When the ram's horn sounds, it signals a call to ascend, to come into the presence of the Almighty, to meet the Lord on the mountain. And then . . . The Test arrives.

Would they do what they promised? Would they risk the smoke and thunder of the mountain? Would they change their hearts and minds to become the kingdom of priests, a "peculiar" people?

The Israelites do not ascend. They hang back, full of fear. They remain at a distance, trembling. In this defining moment, only Moses rises to the challenge, climbing the mountain alone. His solo journey up the mountain stands as a symbol of what it means to heed the call when others falter—a testament to stepping forward when beckoned to higher places. The Israelites don't pass The Test.

When we stop and consider that this is the story of the Lord's covenant people, it's odd, isn't it? Their story is one of failure. I think we tell these stories because they're *our* stories. In them, we can see ourselves, our failures, and our successes. While scripture has examples of success, it also has failures. Because we will fail, the Lord tells stories of people, just like us, who will stumble, take the wrong path, and make mistakes.

Yet, through Jesus Christ, we can succeed. We can pass The Test, ascend, and overcome our doubts and fears. The question is, how?

Zeezrom

An amazing story of The Test is in the book of Alma. The story of Zeezrom is an example of someone who is redeemed after initially failing The Test. This story helps us to understand how, after initial failure, we can learn to have success.

Zeezrom lives in the city of Ammonihah. He's a lawyer and uses his gifts of clever words and logic to debate two missionaries, Alma and Amulek. We read of him, "Now Zeezrom was a man who was expert in the devices of the devil, that he might destroy that which was good" (Alma 11:21). Scripture tells us that Zeezrom was not just confused or tricked but a powerful force for evil. During this time, there were great political dissensions caused by the teachings of Nehor, another clever man, whose ideas infected the people and persuaded them to use religion for gain. These "priestcrafts" manipulated people and tore down the people of God. Zeezrom was a follower of Nehor and an expert in priestcrafts.

Zeezrom first attempts to confound the missionaries by trying to convince Alma and Amulek that Christ won't come. He tries to use logic and debate to tear down their belief in the coming Resurrection. When clever words fail, Zeezrom even tries to bribe them to deny their faith.

Zeezrom uses clever but ultimately untrue ideas to try to persuade the missionaries. He may have used different methods to share his ideas, and he may have used different technology than we have today, but his message is the same. He spews hate and packages it up as truth. He tears down where the gospel raises up. He works to convince others that what Alma and Amulek teach is wrong.

If the story stopped here, we would say Zeezrom failed The Test when presented with the chance to change. On the other hand, Alma and Amulek stay strong and pass their Test, one that Zeezrom creates, but in the story of testing, Zeezrom's Test doesn't end there.

As the debate continues, Zeezrom becomes increasingly troubled by his own actions. As Alma and Amulek see through his deceptions and testify of Christ, Zeezrom's heart softens. And then he *changes*.

> And it came to pass that Zeezrom was astonished at the words which had been spoken; and he also knew concerning the blindness of the minds, which he had caused among the people by his lying words; and his soul began to be harrowed up under a consciousness of his own guilt; yea, he began to be encircled about by the pains of hell.
>
> And it came to pass that he began to cry unto the people, saying: Behold, I am guilty, and these men are spotless before God. And he began to plead for them from that time forth. (Alma 14:6–7)

As Zeezrom's guilt and inner turmoil continue and become so intense that he falls ill. Alma and Amulek encounter Zeezrom in a neighboring city sick with a fever caused by his tormented conscience. Finally, Zeezrom recognizes the error of his ways and the truth of the missionaries' message. He turns to the One who can help him change, and he turns to Alma to help him change. The story picks up with Alma returning to Zeezrom's bedside, saying:

> Believest thou in the power of Christ unto salvation?
> And he answered and said: Yea, I believe all the words that thou hast taught.
> And Alma said: If thou believest in the redemption of Christ thou canst be healed.
> And he said: Yea, I believe according to thy words.
> And then Alma cried unto the Lord, saying: O Lord our God, have mercy on this man, and heal him according to his faith which is in Christ.
> And when Alma had said these words, Zeezrom leaped upon his feet, and began to walk; and this was done to the great astonishment of all the people; and the knowledge of this went forth throughout all the land of Sidom.
> And Alma baptized Zeezrom unto the Lord; and he began from that time forth to preach unto the people. (Alma 15:6–12)

Through the power of Jesus Christ, Zeezrom changes. The man who was originally tearing down the Church, trying to bribe missionaries, becomes a living embodiment of The Test. His journey is more than just change; it's a rebirth. It is a profound testament to the power of faith and the mercy of Christ.

Zeezrom's conversion is a testament to the profound influence of sincere faith and the truths of the gospel. His journey from adversary to disciple highlights the transformative power of the Atonement to change who we are into something greater. The story of Zeezrom doesn't merely end with his physical healing; it is the beginning of a new chapter in his life. With his newfound faith, Zeezrom becomes an ardent advocate for the gospel he once sought to destroy. His story demonstrates that The Test is not just about resisting temptation or overcoming challenges; it's about the inner transformation that occurs when we open our hearts to the truth and allow Christ's Atonement to change us from within.

In Zeezrom, we see a reflection of our own potential for change. His story is a reminder that we are all subject to The Test in various forms throughout our lives. But more importantly, it is a narrative of hope, showing us that failing The Test is not the end. Just as Zeezrom turned his life around, so too can we. No matter the trials we face or the errors we have made, we have hope of changing our character and our inner selves through Him. All of us can be healed, redeemed, and transformed.

The story of Zeezrom gives us a key to understanding how to overcome the trials and tests in our lives. While Zeezrom helps us see the key in action, the Savior teaches it with clarity.

The Prayer

There is another reference to The Test in the New Testament. This example, although well known, is often times overlooked, leading us to miss the reference. It's when the Savior is teaching His followers how to pray. We know this prayer as the Lord's Prayer:

> Our Father which art in heaven, Hallowed be thy name.
> Thy kingdom come. Thy will be done in earth, as it is in heaven.
> Give us this day our daily bread.
> And forgive our debts, as we forgive our debtors.
> *And lead us not into temptation, but deliver us from evil:*

For thine is the kingdom, and the power, and the glory, forever. Amen. (Matthew 6:9–13; emphasis added)

Note that important phrase toward the end: "And lead us not into temptation, but deliver us from evil." In this often repeated and beloved prayer is a direct reference to The Test. Once again, the Lord is reminding us that we are here to be tested and tried. This prayer is a request for mercy as we are being tested, a plea for challenges that are within our capacity to withstand and a supplication for deliverance from the adversary. In these few words, we find an acknowledgment of our continuous struggle and a reminder of our need for the Lord's sustaining hand in every trial we face.

As the Savior and His disciples enter the Garden of Gethsemane, marking the beginning of His Atonement, He alluded to The Test they were about to face, saying, "Pray that you enter not into temptation" (Luke 22:40). Christ foresees the daunting challenges awaiting them—a test of faith amidst fear, confusion, and overwhelming doubt in the dark hours before His Resurrection. The disciples, the Apostles who followed Him, knew Him, and walked their path side by side with Him face their own test over the next few days. He wants them to pray for help and mercy because their own challenges are just beginning.

The Lord's Test

Lastly, the most beautiful and profound example of The Test is epitomized in the Lord's Atonement, a pinnacle of divine challenge and triumph. Where so many of us fail, where we falter in our personal trials, the Savior succeeds; Christ exemplifies the fulfillment of the ultimate Test. He shows us through example the *how* of facing and conquering trials by praying for support as he faces the final fearful events of His life. As He agonizes in the Garden, fully aware of the terrible path that lay ahead, He offers a powerful prayer that resonates with profound faith and submission: "Father, if you are willing, remove this cup from me; yet not my will, but yours be done" (Luke 22:42). In this moment, Christ faces the *nasah* not with defiance but a willingness to embrace the Father's will. This prayer is not a mere acceptance of fate but a testament to His unwavering commitment to the divine plan of salvation. Here in this solitary and solemn moment, the Savior of humanity confronts The Test not by evading the impending suffering but by affirming His complete submission to the Father's will. He is the true example of passing The Test.

Conclusion

In the end, The Test is all about the Savior. He passed through The Test for you and for me. He navigated The Test, the *nasah*, not just for Himself but for all of us, to show us how and support us through our own Tests. Through His example, we learn that by submitting to His will, we can overcome. His assurance "am with you always, even unto the end of the world" (Matthew 28:20) comforts us with the knowledge that we're not alone during our Test. As we turn our hearts to Him, He will help us, and He will never leave us.

He says, "Behold, ye are little children and ye cannot bear all things now; ye must grow in grace and in the knowledge of the truth. Fear not, little children, for you are mine, and I have overcome the world, and you of them that my Father hath given me; And none of them that my Father hath given me shall be lost" (Doctrine and Covenants 50:40–42).

And that is why I weep. When I watch a story of redemption, even a space opera like Star Wars or the story of Gethsemane, I weep at the times when a person passes The Test, when they change, find hope, or reveal who they really are, even after terrible deeds, doubts, and failures.

I am emotional because I hope that I can one day be the person that overcomes—that underneath my rough exterior and beyond my failures, the Lord will help me pass my Test. I cry at these stories because I have hope and faith that one day the Lord will turn to me and say, "I was right about you."

And so it is hope that moves me to tears: hope in the face of life's tests, not just for myself but for everyone struggling through their own trials. I remember that these tests are an integral part of life that have been intentionally included so that we can show Him our love, our devotion, and our character as He showed us His. No matter how many times we may have struggled before, Jesus Christ stands ready to see us through the next Test so that He can trade the all of our struggle for the "all the Father hath."

V
A Periwinkle Purse

By Marianna Richardson

I told my mother everything—my joys, my fears, my frustrations. So when my husband, Steve, received an unexpected phone call inviting us to meet with President Eyring, who then called us to be mission leaders in Brazil, my mom was the first person I called.

I was so excited. I was excited to serve a full-time mission (which I had never done before). I was excited to serve with wonderful young missionaries. I was excited to preach the gospel to the people in Brazil. I was excited about living in another country. I was excited that the Lord had confidence in me and that He thought I could do it! And I knew my mother would be a phone call away to cheer me on.

Then the trials started.

As Steve and I began filling out the paperwork for our mission, we both needed extensive physicals. Steve rarely sees a doctor and rarely gets sick. During his examination, the doctor discovered prostate cancer. Steve would need his prostate removed six weeks before we were to leave for Brazil. I was terrified he wouldn't heal in time or that there would be complications.

I called my mother and she reassured me that all would be well. My father had had the same problem, and she was sure that Steve would heal quickly after the operation. She made the point that we might not have discovered the cancer until much later if it hadn't been for the mission call. Perhaps this was a blessing in disguise.

During these six weeks before we left, we also had a large home to sell. The housing market was robust, and we found a potential buyer quickly. I was busy trying to figure out what belongings to put into storage, what things to give or throw away, and what possessions we would need in Brazil. Suddenly, the housing market changed (this was the spring of 2008). Without warning, the buyer walked away from the sale of our home. The market fell, and there were no new buyers to be found. I felt lost and didn't know what to do. I called my mother again. She told me about the many times she and my father had to move without their home being sold. "All will be well," she assured me. "The Lord will watch out for you."

As I continued to prepare, I remembered what the Prophet Joseph Smith told the early Saints: "Let us cheerfully do all things that lie in our power; and then may we stand still, with the utmost assurance, to see the salvation of God, and for his arm to be revealed" (Doctrine and Covenants 123:17). I prayed for strength and held on to my mother's consoling words. As she had predicted, Steve recovered from the operation without incident. And although our house did not sell until just before our return home from the mission, everything worked out in the end. Wile trying to forget about our then unsold home, I continued preparing for our adventure in Brazil, my previous excitement returning.

The month before we left, Steve and I decided to make a final visit to each of our adult children and grandchildren to say goodbye before we entered the MTC. Our children were scattered across the country, and the trip would take weeks. While I was traveling, my mother went into the hospital to have a pacemaker placed in her heart. The doctors were very hopeful that this operation would enable her to live a more robust life.

We were visiting our daughter Amy, her husband, John, and their three adorable boys in Lafayette, Indiana when I received a phone call from my brother that my mother's heart had stopped on the operating table. They had revived her and hoped she would become stronger as the pacemaker started to work. Years earlier my mother had been in a serious accident that had made her need several operations, and I had not been able to assist her or visit her. This time, I wanted to be by her bedside. This time, I felt like I needed to be there. I immediately hopped on a plane to Salt Lake City and was sitting by her hospital bed within twelve hours of the phone call.

My mother passed away suddenly and peacefully within hours after I arrived. Our entire family was devastated. A light left our lives. All the family attended my mother's funeral. With twelve children, eighty-five grandchildren, and thirty-five great-grandchildren, we were quite an awesome group. All of us were in shock because mother was the glue that held us together. Now we would need to hold ourselves together—closer and more tightly. During the funeral, we hugged, cried, and reminisced together.

The funeral occurred just three weeks before I was to leave for Brazil. Selfishly, I felt abandoned by my mother. I had looked forward to sharing my experiences with her. I knew that no matter how difficult my missionary experience would be, my mother would help me celebrate the good times and understand the bad. Even though I would be in Brazil, she would only be a phone call away. Now that had all changed.

I knew I was just thinking of myself—like when I threw a tantrum as a little girl because my sick father couldn't come with me on a daddy-daughter date. I needed to think about how happy my mother was feeling rather than my own loss. She was reunited with my father who had passed two years earlier. Their reunion would be the epitome of joy.

During the funeral, as I was contemplating my loss, I felt a pit in the bottom of my stomach. It was the first time I could relate to C.S. Lewis's explanation of grief when he said, "No one ever told me that grief felt so like fear. I am not afraid, but the sensation is like being afraid. The same fluttering in the stomach, the same restlessness, the yawning. I keep on swallowing."[10] I felt that same feeling.

---

10. C. S. Lewis, *A Grief Observed* (San Francisco, CA: HarperOne, 1961), 3.

Raising my Ebenezer

My mother's favorite hymn was "Come Thou Font of Every Blessing," which she had asked to be sung at her funeral. As I listened to the words, I began to feel reassurance from the
Lord that He was only a prayer away. I would have His help. I could tell Him of my triumphs and problems, and He would be there to celebrate and console me. The words of the second verse struck deep into my heart:

Here I raise my Ebenezer
Here by Thy great help I've come
And I hope by Thy good pleasure
Safely to arrive at home [11]

When I returned home, I decided to study the phrase "raise my Ebenezer." It is a concept briefly mentioned in 1 Samuel 5:1 and 7:12. At that time, the people of Israel had recently lost the ark of the covenant in a battle with the Philistines. Eli, the high priest, was so distraught by the loss that he fell off his seat backwards and broke his neck. So, Samuel became the new spiritual leader of the Israelite nation. He encouraged the people to turn to the Lord in their time of difficulty saying, "Prepare your hearts unto the Lord and serve him only" (1 Samuel 7:3).

Even though the Philistines had won the battle, bad things were happening to them because they had taken Israel's sacred ark and placed it with their idols of stone. The stone statue of Dagon mysteriously fell and smashed into pieces. All the people in the city where the ark of the covenant was kept broke out in huge boils. Without any compulsion from the Israelites, the Philistines returned the ark with a peace offering of five golden mice and five gold emerods, which were a representation of the painful boils the God of Israel had cursed them with.

But the covenant people's troubles did not end there. The Israelites gathered to worship together, rejoicing over the ark's return. When the Philistines heard about it, they decided to exact their revenge. As

---

11. John Wyeth, "Come Thou Fount of Every Blessing," https://www.churchofjesuschrist.org/music/text/other/come-thou-fount-of-every-blessing?lang=eng.

the Philistines came to battle a second time, "the Lord thundered with a great thunder" (1 Samuel 7:10), which so confused the Philistines that they were easy prey for the Israelites.

Because of the Lord's help, this enemy of Israel was subdued and stopped battling against the Israelites.

In gratitude and in remembrance of all the Lord had done for them, Samuel took a stone he called "Eben-ezer," which in Hebrew means "stone of help." He positioned it at the place of the battle to remind the people of this great miracle. The children of Israel now had a token to remind them of His power, His grace, and His miracles. And I began to feel that way, too.

Celebrate Life

After the funeral, I had three weeks to finish my preparations. I tried to deal with my grief by keeping busy. While packing boxes and deciding what to take and what to put into storage, I began to think about the lessons my mother had taught me. My heart began to heal and change. One particular story stuck out in my mind. This experience had changed my mother and her perspective on life. Remembering it helped me to start replacing my pain with joy.

My mother was in her early fifties, enjoying the freedom of being an empty nester. One bright summer's day, she was walking home from shopping trip and stopped at a light. When the pedestrian sign blinked green, she started into the crosswalk just as a young man decided to make a right hand turn on the red light. He had been looking at the cars coming from the opposite direction and forgot to check for any pedestrians crossing the street. He hit the gas pedal while hurriedly turning into the street, trying to make it before the oncoming cars.

The car hit her knees and caused her to crumple and fall. The screams of onlookers caused the driver to hit the brake inches from her head. During the subsequent months, she was in and out of hospitals for various operations to fix her damaged body and smashed lower leg.

Doctors were not sure if she would ever be able to walk again. After a few of the operations, she experienced serious complications and indescribable pain. This was no miraculous healing. After long months and years of physical therapy, she was able to walk with a limp, but her knee and leg often caused her pain, being swollen and tender until the day she died.

She could have felt sorry for herself. She could have become depressed. She could have become emotionally stuck on the question: "How could the Lord let this happen to me?" Instead, she stopped herself from asking that question and focused on a new one. She began to ask herself: "What does the Lord want me to learn from this experience?" She learned many lessons from her painful experiences and wrote her inspired thoughts in a book called, "Celebration!"

Her words healed my heart:

> Celebration is the conscious decision to live our lives with joy. In the midst of turmoil, pain, and adversity, in bad times and good, joy is the great companion our Heavenly Father intended us to have. To feel joy, however, requires a decision on our part—a chosen approach to life, a chosen attitude, a constant awareness. This decision is the necessary beginning to recognizing, feeling, and developing the joy with which Heavenly Father has filled our creation. Anyone can live with a sense of celebration . . . Celebration is self-made.[12]

It was up to me to feel the joy of my new calling. My mother would be with me in other ways. And as I turned my heart more fully to the Lord, my sense of loss and depression was lessened, even though I still missed her deeply.

The Periwinkle Purse

Just before leaving, my siblings gathered and chose the things they wanted to keep from our parent's possessions. I looked at the many items of beauty and value that I could choose from, and I decided to choose something that would be a symbol of help to me. It would be my Ebenezer stone while I served my mission to remind me of my mother's faith and my own faith in the gospel of Jesus Christ.

I chose her periwinkle purse.

I felt that having her purse constantly on my arm would be a token of my mother and the things she taught me. Though the bright colors

---

12. Jaroldeen A. Edwards, *Celebration: 10 Principles of More Joyous Living* (Salt Lake City, UT: Deseret Book, 1995), 3.

rarely coordinated with my missionary outfits, I loved that purse. It not only helped me to heal, but it opened my mind to new lessons during the many years I carried it. Carrying the purse reminded me of the way my mother used her purse to serve others.

But my heart was still in pain. I began to think about the lessons my mother learned from pain. Her words came into my mind: "The first thing we must do in order to begin to gain the lessons from pain is to accept what is past and let it go."[13] I resolved to let go of my pain and to focus on my mission. I knew that was what the Lord (and my mother) wanted me to do.

The Trial of Learning a Language

When we arrived in Brazil, my trials continued. The biggest trial for me was that my Portuguese was very minimal. I could not understand anything anyone said. Some words here and there sounded familiar, but most of the words did not sound anything like the Portuguese I had been studying. I was at a complete loss as to what was going on around me. My inability to communicate was a problem if I wanted to preach the gospel to a Brazilian or help a Brazilian missionary.

Learning Portuguese continued to be difficult for me even though I loved the Portuguese language. It sounds so beautiful! But I had never really learned a foreign language before, except for high school French thirty-five years previously (and I wasn't very good at French back then either). I had tried to practice Portuguese in the few months before we left, but I had so much to do and so many problems to take care of that I needed every second just to prepare to leave home. Now in Brazil, I realized how powerful words were, and my lack of words made me feel powerless.

At our first zone conference, I brought the periwinkle purse. I laid it by my chair and stood at the pulpit to give my first well-prepared talk in Portuguese. I had practiced it many times out loud, trying to say all the words correctly. A Brazilian missionary who spoke English and Portuguese came up to me afterward and said, "Sister Richardson,

---

13. Edwards, *Celebration*, 60.

I felt the Spirit while you were talking, but I couldn't understand a word you said." That was hard to hear!

Rather than be discouraged, I became more determined to speak Portuguese so that my missionaries and the Brazilian Saints would know how much I love and appreciate them, their country, their culture, and most importantly, the gospel. But I knew I needed to do something more.

I prayed very hard for answers. The Lord inspired me many times with Portuguese words beyond my ability to speak. I found a tutor who helped me translate and practice my talks before I gave them. My husband, who is a linguist and whose Portuguese is flawless, would have me say my talks in the car as we drove from chapel to chapel, and he would say the words so I could hear them correctly spoken, which helped me become more understandable.

I found comfort in the scriptures. Alma told his son Helaman, "For I do know that whosoever shall put their trust in God shall be supported in their trials, and their troubles, and their afflictions, and shall be lifted up at the last day" (Alma 36:3). I did feel supported by the Spirit and wasn't emotionally distressed, but I was still struggling with the language. There was no immediate miracle. Like my mother's long journey of healing after her accident, I didn't experience a miraculous gift-of-tongues moment. With my mother's purse by my side, I was reminded to look to her example for help. My mother had faced trials much more difficult than mine during her life. Through pondering, I realized that I had a choice to view learning the language either as an opportunity to learn and grow, or as an insurmountable obstacle that only brought frustration into an already stressful situation.

I remembered how my mother always used the word "Glorious!" to describe everything around her. Her children were glorious. Her friends were glorious. The sun was glorious. The food was glorious. And, of course, the gospel was glorious too. That one word said a lot about my mother and about how she felt about everything. All she had to do was say that one word—"Glorious!"—and that was sufficient to lift her mood and the mood of those around her. It was not putting on a mask; it was an effort to find joy in the moment.

The concept of rejoicing amid trials can be found repeatedly throughout the scriptures. Moses on Mount Sinai told the tribes of

Israel to "rejoice in all that you put your hand unto" (Deuteronomy 12:7). Isaiah prophesied that "the meek also shall increase their joy in the Lord, and the poor among men shall rejoice in the Holy One of Israel" (Isaiah 29:19). In the book of Luke, Jesus spoke to those who were persecuted for his name, saying, "Rejoice ye in that day, and leap for joy: for, behold, your reward is great in heaven" (Luke 6:23).

At the last supper, Jesus taught, "In the world ye shall have tribulation: but be of good cheer; I have overcome the world" (John 16:33). And Nephi, after feeling the bitterness of anger in his heart while struggling with his wicked brothers, changed his attitude by saying, "Awake, my soul! No longer droop in sin. Rejoice, O my heart, and give place no more for the enemy of my soul" (2 Nephi 4:28).

I decided to pick a positive and affirming word that could be easily understood in both English and Portuguese—a word that would bring immediate joy to the listener. Saying this word would be my way of rejoicing in the good things around me, even while I continued to struggle with the language. So I picked the word "Woohoo!" as a way of expressing my excitement for missionary work and for my missionaries. Whenever I said "Woohoo!" I felt better. It was my way of saying, "I love being a missionary here in Brazil! I love the Lord! I love the missionaries! Woohoo, the gospel's true!" The phrase even rhymes in Portuguese: "Woohoo, o evangelho é verdadeiro!"

That single word reminded me of all the positive feelings I initially experienced for my calling as a missionary. Even when I felt frustrated, sad, depressed, or tired, I found great power in saying the single word "Woohoo!" Not only did it make me feel better, but it made my missionaries feel better too. They knew I was proud of them when I said "Woohoo!" after a baptism. They knew I cared about them when I said "Woohoo!" after they called me to tell me they were healthy following an illness. They knew I was excited to be with them and serve with them when I said "Woohoo!" as I passed them on the streets of São Paulo or during a district meeting or zone meeting.

I remember the first time I used the word "Woohoo!" in a stake conference talk. I told the Brazilian Saints the story of my mother being hit by a car and her words about celebration. Then I explained my difficulties learning Portuguese and how I found my own word for celebration, and I let out a "Woohoo!" Everyone looked up at me immediately in surprise. Many of the children had incredulous smiles on their faces. After the meeting, I had both children and adults alike give me a hug and just say a single word: "Woohoo!" My favorite memory is walking down the hallway of the São Paulo temple dressed in white, headed for an endowment session. Another lovely sister temple worker was walking toward me. I was surprised to hear her whisper "Woohoo!" as she passed me in the hallway.

The power of woohoo expresses joy in the gospel, even during trials. The English word *gospel* literally means "good news." The Savior calls His message to the world "good tidings of great joy" (Luke 2:10). Great joy is better than mere happiness. Worldly happiness is fleeting and ephemeral, lasting but a moment before it's gone. Joy is endless happiness, or God's happiness, for *Endless* is one of His names (see Doctrine and Covenants 19:10).

The Joyful Songs of Women

As I studied the scriptures more thoroughly, I was surprised to discover that women expressed their praise for the Lord through songs of joy. Five righteous women's songs are recorded in the Bible. The first to sing was Miriam, the sister of Moses. She watched over her baby brother's basket when Moses was set afloat as an infant in the River Nile. When Moses returned as a prophet to Egypt, Miriam was by Moses's side as he battled with Pharaoh to let the Israelites go. Right after the Egyptian army was drowned in the depths of the Red Sea, Miriam gathered the women together and said, "Sing ye to the Lord, for he hath triumphed gloriously" (Exodus 15:20–21). (I have secretly wondered if my mother borrowed the word *glorious* from Miriam.)

About two hundred years later, the Israelites were established in the promised land, but they were still fighting to maintain their borders. Barak, the head of the Israelite army, asked Deborah, a prophetess, to join him in leading his men to battle. Deborah warned Barak that if he did not fulfill his calling valiantly and vanquish the enemy, a woman would be praised as the vanquisher instead of him. God miraculously was on the side of Israel, and the enemy soon retreated. The enemy's captain ran for his life, hiding in a woman's tent. Jael, the woman who lived in the tent, gave him a drink, which put him to sleep. She then ended his life by piercing his temple with a tent stake.

(Boy, what a headache!) At their victory celebration, Deborah sang her song, praising the Lord and Jael: "I, even I, will sing unto the Lord; I will sing praise to the Lord God of Israel. . . . Blessed above women shall Jael . . . be, blessed shall she be above women in the tent. . . . O Lord: but let them that love him be as the sun when he goeth forth in his might" (Judges 5:1, 24, 31).

Hannah was the mother of Samuel. Her son would become the prophet during the reigns of King Saul and King David. She sang a song of rejoicing at a particularly difficult time when she was giving up her son to God. Originally, she thought she would never be a mother because she had been barren for many years. With heartache and pain, she prayed at the temple gates for a child, saying, "Remember me and not forget thine handmaiden" (1 Samuel 1:11). Hannah promised that if the Lord would grant her this wish, she would return her son to God and have him serve God all his days. After weaning the child, she brought young Samuel to the temple and was overcome by the Spirit. Her song at this time of great sacrifice was one of joy and prophecy. She sang, "My heart rejoiceth in the Lord. . . . My mouth is enlarged over my enemies . . . because I rejoice in thy salvation. There is none holy as the Lord . . . neither is there any rock like our God" (1 Samuel 2:1–2).

One thousand years later, a pregnant Mary traveled to her cousin Elizabeth, who also carried a precious son conceived through God's help. Elizabeth felt the baby leap within her and proclaimed Mary's child to be the Christ: "Blessed art thou among women and blessed is the fruit of thy womb. And whence is this to me, that the mother of my Lord should come to me? For, lo, as soon as the voice of thy salutation sounded in mine ears, the babe leaped in my womb for joy" (Luke 1:42–44). Elizabeth's song-like proclamation must have brought such comfort to Mary as another witness of the mission of her future son. Perhaps during this time, Mary was worried about Joseph's and other people's reactions to her pregnancy. Mary needed this reassurance from her beloved older relative whom she admired.

Elizabeth's words seem to have inspired the mother of Christ to sing as well. Mary's song began with words very similar to Hannah's song. She also called herself a handmaiden and then sang, "My soul doth magnify the Lord, And my spirit hath rejoiced in God my

Saviour" (Luke 1:46–47). Then Mary touched on multiple prophecies about Christ, confirmed that He will fulfill them, and added her own prophecy about His mission: "He hath filled the hungry with good things; and the rich he hath sent away empty" (Luke 1:53). She ended with saying that Jesus will "give light to them that sit in darkness" and "guide our feet into the way of peace" (Luke 1:79). This light in the darkness is the foundation of finding joy through tribulation; it's seeing the good through the eyes of the Spirit, even when things aren't easy. This light in the midst of despair is something to sing about!

I have felt this great joy as I have worked to understand the "good news" of Jesus Christ. His message is that He, Jesus Christ, came to earth and suffered the imperfections, pains, and sins of all mankind. Through His Atonement, all mankind may be saved through obedience to the laws and ordinances of the gospel. Death has lost its sting because all of us will be resurrected! Through repentance and eternal covenants, all of us will have the opportunity to choose to return to Heavenly Father once more!

When I review my trials, such as the death of my mother or my inability to learn Portuguese, they seem so small in comparison to the miracle of the gospel. As I consider these powerful women who sang songs of joy, even with their challenges, I am inspired to sing all the more. Then I remember Alma's stirring question: "If ye have felt to sing the song of redeeming love, I would ask, can ye feel so now?" (Alma 5:26).

For me, the answer is yes! Through the Lord, I know that all my efforts will be enough even if I never succeed perfectly. I know the Lord will guide me and use my talents as he sees fit.

He is my hope!

He is my joy!

He is my salvation!

Woohoo, the gospel's true!

VI

Finding Freedom in Prison

By Portia Louder

I spent four and a half years in federal prison. It was summertime in Minnesota when I arrived at the prison; the weather was beautiful, and I found a place under a tree in the rec yard that became my sanctuary. I spent a lot of time under that tree. I went outside during the day to feel connected to God.

One morning as I thought about my children growing up without me, the pain seemed more than I could bear. I was so far away from home, and the distance seemed overwhelming! As I got up to leave, one of my coworkers offered these comforting words:

"Portia, maybe you're feeling weak right now, but I see your incredible strength. I know you're struggling, and I want you to know that you're not alone; you were never alone. We love you. I've been praying for you, and there are people who love you and want you to succeed, both in heaven and on earth."

Her words comforted my soul. I needed to know that God was mindful of me. She pointed to a planter that was nearby and said,

"Aren't these flowers beautiful? You know, they have to die each year so they can be reborn."

My tears flowed freely.

"You will get through this, and someday you will teach people how to go through their own rebirth, because you will have already experienced it. You are in a good place to help others. Embrace it."

I thought about my coworker's words all afternoon. I admired her; she was a disciplined woman, a great writer and communicator, and her strength and willingness to serve others was inspiring.

Later that day while I was sitting in the commissary, I remembered a dream I had before I was sentenced. I felt vulnerable and scared and thought I could hear my children's voices. I knew they needed me, and I was terrified to leave them. Now I remembered the dream differently; I saw it from a new perspective. I could hear their voices, and they were happy. They took turns calling out to me. My oldest daughter, Shelby, said, "Mom needs us, but she won't let us help her. I'm going to send CJ in to get her."

I could see myself sitting in a jail cell alone, and I wouldn't leave. CJ walked in and grabbed my hand. "Come on, Mom, let's go; we're all waiting for you." CJ giggled, which is one of my favorite sounds, and we walked out together. I was free!

I could see that I had choices. I could choose to use my time wisely. I could choose to serve others. I could choose to be a positive and uplifting influence in my children's lives. I could choose my response to the situation I was in. I could choose to be free on the inside.

That evening when I went to the cafeteria to eat dinner, I noticed a woman staring at me as she was mopping the floor. I smiled at her, and she said, "You're glowing!"

She was Hispanic; English was her second language, and I wasn't sure if I heard her right. I said, "I'm new to this compound. My name is Portia."

"Your face is glowing, friend. I can see the light all around you," she said. "God will bless you when you leave prison because you're here for us."

It was a strange comment, but strange things happen quite often in prison, so I thanked her and went on my way.

The next morning there was a cool breeze as I walked around the track. The sky was blue, and the trees seemed to dance with color. I felt peace as I thought about my children. I felt honored to be their mother. I noticed beauty in the simple things around me.

I said a prayer. "Father, I am willing to let go of everything I am. I don't have much to give, but everything I thought I was and everything I wanted to be is Yours if You will have it. I know You love me, and I believe in miracles. I want to be a new woman; please heal me."

That was the day I was reborn.

I chose to take responsibility for the choices I made, and God gave me the power to move forward. I made a list of everything I had done to hurt anyone. I wrote an outline of my life, using main events, characters, and key experiences to create a spreadsheet. I started with honesty and created categories. I went by age and listed everyone I could think of who I had harmed. It took me a few months, and when I got done, I felt like I had accomplished something monumental. As I made my list, I was able to look back at my life in a more objective way, without judgment. The painful feelings I carried turned into love. I had compassion for myself, the people I hurt, and the people who had hurt me. I had a strong desire to reach out and make things right.

I shared everything on my list with a group of trusted friends. Then I went to the rec yard, and I buried my list.

I cannot emphasize enough how much this experience changed my life. I took full ownership, and it gave me freedom! After I buried my sins in the rec yard, my life began to change. I started dreaming about my future again. I saw my life differently; my heart opened, and the love I felt for others was magnified. I felt power come into my life, and I was able to rewrite my story. I had the strongest desire to help people heal and grow.

I wanted to validate the pain I had caused my family and my community. I wrote letters apologizing and asked them to share their feelings with me. I faced the truth and surrendered my will to God.

I had great roommates in prison, and I was especially close to one of my roommates named Sonia. Sonia's first language was Spanish. When I moved into our cell, Sonia asked if I would read with her so she could learn more English. We spent a lot of time together and became close friends. I felt a calming influence around Sonia. I looked forward to reading together, and I appreciated the peace I felt when I was in our room.

Sonia told me she prayed for me every night when I first moved in. "You were strong, but you needed patience and peace," she said. "I asked God to comfort you."

When I got to the prison in Minnesota, most of the women on the floor of our unit were quiet and respectful of others. That changed six months later when our unit counselor moved ten women into a large cell across from ours.

The new women stayed up late at night laughing and listening to loud music, not seeming to care how their behavior impacted the rest of us. They made homemade speakers and attached them to radios and headphones to amplify the sound.

After a couple of weeks, my roommates asked if I would talk to them. "Please, Miss Portia, ask them to keep the noise down. They're so loud and disrespectful that no one can sleep."

Those kinds of conversations don't usually go very well in prison, so I decided to pray instead. I prayed every night that peace would be restored, but things only got worse.

One night as I was praying, it occurred to me that these women were my neighbors, and I hadn't made any effort to get to know them. I was praying for them to change their behavior, and I hadn't considered that I needed to change my heart.

The next day I went to their cell and spent time talking to my neighbors. I looked at pictures of their families and loved ones and started praying to recognize their divine potential.

That's when things began to change.

Late one evening, they asked if I would say a prayer with them; one of the women in their room was having a hard time. Afterward, they apologized for being too loud and told me they would keep the noise down.

When I saw them on the compound, they waved and seemed happy to see me.

We became friends.

In time, I came to know my neighbors' stories; I loved them and was saddened by the burdens they had to carry.

Mother Teresa said, "We have forgotten that we belong to each other."[14] In prison I learned that we truly do belong to each other.

On August 7, 2019, almost four and a half years after my husband Chad dropped me off at a federal prison, he sat waiting in the parking lot of the Victorville, California, prison compound to pick me up.

It was 7:30 in the morning, and it was already getting hot outside. I decided to wear my gray prison shorts and my best white T-shirt. I bought the white T-shirt from a girl for five dollars (we don't have money in prison, so I paid her with two bags of potato chips), and I had been saving it for almost a year to wear home. I woke up early and used a blow-dryer on my hair. I put on the wet-and-wild eyeshadow and lipstick that I bought in prison at the Commissary and used only on special occasions.

I was excited and nervous! I was going home; I was leaving so much behind! I walked through the unit one last time, and a close friend stopped to give me a hug.

When I walked back to my bunk, my friend Maisie was waiting for me.

"I don't want to cry, Portia, because I'm really happy for you, but I'm going to miss you so much. You were the first person I met when I got to prison. I've done all my time with you, and I don't know what it's going to be like without you."

She started to cry, then I started to cry. "Let's pray, Maisie."

"Father in Heaven," I prayed. "We love Thee and call upon the powers of heaven to comfort and protect us as we say goodbye. Give us peace and wrap Maisie in the arms of Thy love when I'm gone. Connect our hearts until we meet again, I pray, in the name of Jesus Christ, amen."

Maisie gave me a hug and said, "I love you, Portia. Let me walk you out."

We sat outside together waiting to hear my name called over the intercom. We laughed at silly things and waited to say goodbye. All

---

14. "Mother Teresa Reflects on Working toward Peace," The Markkula Center for Applied Ethics, accessed Mar. 16, 2024, https://www.scu.edu/mcae/architects-of-peace/Teresa/essay.html.

of my earthly possessions fit neatly into a cardboard box; everything important was inside my heart.

"LOUDER" came across the intercom.

"That's me!"

"That's you, Portia. Let's go," Maisie said.

Maisie walked me to the front of the building, and she sat on a bench and waved as I got in the car with my husband, Chad, and rode away.

I sat quietly looking out the window and held my husband's hand.

The world seemed so big, and I didn't know what to say.

Chad said, "I can't believe you're really here sitting next to me."

When I looked at him, I felt something so tender. This man had sacrificed so much for me and our family! How I love him.

If I could go back and give myself something, it would be these two lessons:

The first lesson: even though you can't see it yet, the hard things you're going through have the ability to transform your life.

Being open to the beauty and willing to consider that there is a reason for the pain allows us to transform our lives. When I was willing to walk through the pain, even the pain that seemed impossible to walk through, I found that there was something beautiful on the other side.

There will be painful moments in life that change your entire world in the matter of minutes. Let them make you stronger and kinder. Let them crack your soul wide open so the light can get in.

The second lesson: there is absolute value in honesty. Being honest with my feelings, honest with myself, and honest with others has brought power into my life. Honesty is one of the highest forms of respect for yourself and others.

I was sitting in church with my husband not long after I got home from prison, and the young children were invited to the front of the chapel to sing. My heart was tender as I thought about one of my own daughters at that age. I remembered her fun personality and felt close to her.

During my time in prison, I missed her growing-up years. My daughter was hurting and I wondered why she couldn't see how amazing she was. Then I remembered how I felt when I was her age,.

Chapter vi: Finding Freedom in Prison

My heart ached, and I prayed, "Please hold my child in the palm of Your hand. I can't do this." Then these words came into my heart: "Portia, you are a daughter of the Most High God. You are a mother and a queen; don't forget who you are! She is mine too. She is becoming who she was born to be."

I lay in bed that night with my daughter and said, "I know you're struggling, and I know that what you're going through is hard. But I also know who you are—you are a daughter of the Most High God, and you were born to be brave!"

I started working with teenagers who had been in and out of foster care. One day I asked the girls in our group to pick a positive word that they could focus on all week. Some of their words were *strong*, *honest*, and *brave*. As I went around the room, one of the girls looked down when it was her turn to pick a word. I asked, "Is there a word you can think of that most embodies who you want to be?"

She said, "Good. I just want to be good."

I told her, "You *are* good." She looked away. When she looked back at me, I looked into her beautiful brown eyes and said, "You *are* good, sweet girl. You're so good!"

I read a Facebook post a while ago about people in prison that said, "They're just the same as us."

The words *they* and *us* were confusing to me. I thought, "That comment would have felt better to me if it would have said, 'We're all the same.'"

Then I realized: we're not all the same. My sweet friend in foster care is braver than I am.

Coming to know your worth doesn't just change you. It changes the way you see everyone else because you can see their worth too.

One morning I sat in silence with a woman who was struggling with addiction.

It was peaceful as the sun came up. We were enjoying the beauty of the earth as we sat on the porch and listened to the birds welcome a new day. I asked my friend, "What made you decide to seek help with your addiction?"

She told me, "I was scared. I thought I could die if I didn't quit using drugs."

I told her, "I'm glad. Now, can I tell you how much you have to look forward to? Recovery is amazing! You'll be more compassionate because of your experiences, and you'll probably enjoy the simple things more. I love the feeling of the sun on my face. My life is so much better than I could have hoped for. Sitting here with you right now fills my heart with joy!"

"Really?" she said. "Will I really be happy again? Because I can't see it right now."

"Let me see it for you then, friend, because I see beauty all around you."

I found out that when everything is taken from you, and there is nothing else to lose, you can focus on changing everything about yourself, and the old version of you becomes your motivation.

Many of us in prison are people who have time to sit, think, analyze, and process our actions. Many of us found our way to recovery. There is power in no longer hiding who we are from the world.

A friend recently asked me what changed the most while I was in prison, and I told him, "I did!" I know that God lives and has compassion for all of His children; His love transformed my life!

The time I spent in prison helped me figure out what really mattered.

I'm grateful that I had the opportunity to live with women from all different cultures and faiths, and I'm grateful to live in Utah with many members of the Church. I used to worry a lot about what other people thought of me; now I just want to live worthy of the experiences I've had.

When I finally let go of the life I thought I was going to live, I found out that God had something grander waiting for me. I know Jesus Christ. I what it feels like to kneel before Him. He is my Savior and my King. When we know who we are and how our Father in Heaven loves us, we can do really hard things.

VII
The Three Goodbyes
By Michelle Wilson

I said goodbye to my mother three times before she died.

We knew it was coming, her death. Mom had been sick for years. But the last few months had been an especially rough time—illness punctuated by strokes. So when I got the news in June of 2020 that her time was quickly coming to an end, I was ready. I called the airlines, packed my bag, and was on a plane to California three hours later. I didn't want her to die before I could say goodbye.

Funny the things you remember. I can't recall how I got to the airport, if there was turbulence, who I sat by, or what complimentary soda I ordered. But I can still feel the sting of the tears I tried to hold back as I asked the person behind the ticket counter for a seat closest to the front of the plane so I could be the first to disembark. I can still feel my heart pounding against my chest as I sat in the third row, rehearsing in my mind what would soon happen: My brother would pick me up at the airport and take me the hospital where Mom was lying in the emergency room. I would hold her hand, kiss her on the cheek, and say goodbye as she drifted toward heaven.

Time felt different. Slow. Fast. Elastic. Angry. The plane couldn't fly fast enough, and yet I wanted it to slow down. I was ready to say goodbye . . . wasn't I?

My brother drove me to the hospital as planned. Due to COVID restrictions, the staff allowed only one person at a time to be with Mom.

When it was my turn, the nurse led me to her bed in a semi-private ER room. She looked different—older than the mom I'd seen just a month before when I'd helped her and Dad move into their new home that would suit her physical condition better.

For a moment, I hesitated. I can't say why.

I stepped into her room and sat by her bed. She smiled. I held her hand and kissed her soft cheek. I told her she was beautiful. I told her I was proud of her. I told her I loved her.

Then my turn was over. I had to leave, but she was still there.

I was prepared to say goodbye. I was prepared for her to leave.

But I wasn't prepared for me to leave her first.

I inhaled courage and kissed her and told her I would see her again someday. Then I said goodbye. I left the room and cried.

She was expected to pass that night. But she didn't. By some miracle the doctors couldn't explain, Mom not only didn't die, but she got out of bed and was talking. She seemed to be improving.

Hope can be a dangerous thing—not something I wanted to embrace in that moment. I had seen her the day before. I knew what was coming. I was prepared.

They moved her to the ICU—an upgrade from the ER, we were told—so she could continue to improve. Unlike the ER, the ICU did not allow visitors. And so we waited for her to either get well enough or sick enough for the hospital to let us see her.

It didn't take long.

That night we got the call. It was time to say goodbye. Again.

I rushed to her bedside. She was awake yet pale, half here and half somewhere else. She smiled. I held her hand. I sang a song to her. I told her I loved her.

The staff allowed more family to be in the room, as it seemed she was dying now.

Chapter VII: The Three Goodbyes

Each of her children and grandchildren said their goodbyes. I stayed in the room, discreetly taking precious pictures and videos for remembrance's sake. I thought I was prepared for that night.

But being prepared doesn't always prepare you for what's coming. Like when my father bent over her and stroked her cheek—they smiled at each other and for a moment had the faces of young love, forever love. Or how Mom would have moments of lucidity and say something so touching and so profound. Or how, when everyone had left, I laid next to her, pulled my face mask off, lay cheek to cheek with her, and said goodbye this time for real.

Leaving her this time was even worse and somehow better. The reality of our separation was so heavy and clear and imminent, and yet there was nothing left unsaid—no love lost. I had closure. Still, I left her side and cried.

But Mom didn't die that night.

In fact, she took another turn for the better the next morning. We were told we could see her if she continued to improve or took another turn for the worse. And so we waited. But not for long. She took a dive for the worst the next day. They moved her to an empty room on the third floor where nurses could take hospice measures. They now allowed visitors again, but only one at a time.

It was almost midnight that next day when I walked toward Mom's hospital room for my turn. Again, I hesitated at the door. But this time I knew why. I didn't want to say goodbye again. I didn't want to see her this way. I didn't want to feel the pain again. I was exhausted emotionally and physically. It was going to be hard. Maybe too hard. I wanted to see her one more time, but I didn't know if I could.

Not too long before that moment of hesitation, I had struggled with a different heavy burden, one I didn't want to face for similar reasons—it was difficult and it hurt. I prayed for strength and support. But mostly I prayed that the situation would go away.

As I prayed, I felt an unexpected prompting: *The Garden of Gethsemane.*

I opened my scriptures to Mark's account of the Savior: "And they came to a place which was named Gethsemane: and he saith to his disciples, Sit ye hear while I shall pray. And he taken with him Peter and James and John, and began to be sore amazed, and to be very heavy. And said unto them, My soul is exceeding sorrowful unto death: tarry ye here, and watch" (Mark 14:32–34).

The Savior was entering a difficult experience (perhaps the greatest understatement of all). His pain was so deep and so heavy that He, the Lord of lords, was astonished by it. He could have stopped there. He could have turned around. But He walked into the pain.

"And he went forth a little, and fell on the ground and prayed that, if it were possible, the hour might pass from him. And he said, Abba, Father, all things are possible unto thee; take away this cup from me: nevertheless not that I will, but what though wilt" (Mark 14:35–36).

I nearly stopped reading. As I read this, I felt this prayer deeply. *Please, Father, take this burden from me. I can't do this. I don't want to do this.* Nevertheless . . .

That's such a power word—nevertheless. It's the trading of my will for His, the ultimate mortal acquiescence. This was the answer I thought I was being given—I can pray for my want, but I must accept His will.

Keep reading, I heard.

Curious, I did.

"And he cometh, and findeth them sleeping, and saith unto Peter, Simon, sleepest thou? couldest not thou watch one hour? Watch ye and pray, lest ye enter into temptation. The spirit truly is ready, but the flesh is weak" (Mark 14:37–38).

That must be my answer. I need to watch more and pray more so I won't be tempted to fear or complain.

Keep reading.

"And again he went away, and prayed" (Mark 14:39).

And there it hit me.

Jesus Christ walked into the garden and felt the weight of the Atonement press on Him in an astonishing way, and yet He *kept* walking into the garden—into the pain. He came out and spoke to His disciples, and He could have stayed with His friends or even left the garden. But He chose to *walk back into the pain.*

Looking up from my scriptures, I wondered what kind of strength that took—to purposely walk into a situation where pain would be inevitable. But I didn't have to wonder why He did it. He did it for us, for me, for love.

Walking into the pain was the only way to give us what we need. It was the only way to save us. He did it because His why was bigger than His pain.

In that moment, I realized that there was and would still be times in my life when I would be spared pain and discomfort. And yet there would be times—like in the moment with my mom—that I needed to walk into the pain because the why would be bigger than the pain.

Back at the hospital, I placed my hand on the door of Mom's room and took in a deep breath. I wanted to see her again. To tell her I love her again. To say goodbye to her a third time—a last time. I opened the door and walked into the pain.

Mom was gray. Gaunt. The sparkle that was in her eyes the day before was gone. The hint of a smile—of life—that had pulled at the corner of her mouth was gone was well. Mom was there, but she was nearly gone too.

I sat on the side of her bed and held her hand. It wasn't as soft and warm as it was during our first goodbye. I stroked her cheek. She didn't smile like she did on our second goodbye.

I talked to her, sang to her. Every once in a while, she would whisper something I couldn't understand. Once she looked at me and smiled and sighed. She was still there. I wasn't prepared for that either.

Once again, time took different shapes. It was slow, fast, elastic. But not angry. It was tender and sad and, yes, painful.

As I laid my head on Mom's chest, something inside me knew this was the last goodbye. I listened to her uneven breathing. She put her hand on my head. And I cried.

Even in pain, God's tender mercies can be found.

As Mom stroked my hair, suddenly, in a clear and vibrant voice, she said my name. I popped up to see her lucid and looking past me. I asked her to tell me what she was looking at, expecting her to say that she was seeing her mom or dad or even a light. Her eyes landed on mine and in a slow and tender voice, she said, "You have great eyebrows."

I surprised myself with a loud laugh. Mom smiled. She was there: my funny mom, with a twinkle in her eye and a smile on her face. And then her face faded back to gray as her eyes clouded over again.

Just then, my phone buzzed. It was 2 a.m. My brother was waiting to take his shift.

I kissed Mom one last time. "I will see you again, Mom," I said.

She smiled weakly at me and nodded. I smiled back. We both knew.

I walked to the door and turned to see her one last time. "Goodbye, Mom," I said for the third time. "I love you."

And then I walked away from her for the last time.

She died ten hours later with Dad by her side.

I often wonder what it would have been like to say goodbye to Mom just once. Or just twice. Or not at all.

Each time I said goodbye, it was harder. Each time I walked into her room, I was walking into the pain.

But each time was sweeter.

I marvel at how the Lord works. How sometimes He provides experiences that are difficult, even painful, because He knows the tender mercies that are there waiting for us.

Mom has been gone a few years now. And now there's a different kind of pain—grief.

I did not walk into that pain at first. I yelled at it. I bartered with it. I ignored it. I called it names—inconvenient, stupid, and even rude.

But over the years, I've learned that I need to walk into the grief too.

I'm sure that looks differently for everyone. But for me, it looks like letting the tears fall when they come. Not feeling weak for missing her. Not feeling shame for being angry.

It looks like dismissing the regrets I can't change and embracing the memories I cherish.

This is something I've learned about walking into the pain. I never walk into the pain alone. When Jesus suffered in the garden He choose to enter, "there appeared an angel unto him from heaven, strengthening him" (Luke 22:43).

Someone once said that grief is love reaching to heaven. I believe that, because when I walk into the pain of a friend, when the veil is thin, I can feel heaven reaching down to me.

In fact, some of my most tender moments with my Father in Heaven have been during my most painful moments. Not all, mind you. Pain isn't required to access Him or His love, thank goodness. I have had many wonderful experiences with God during my happy times as well. But when life calls upon us to walk into the pain for a greater *why*, He is right there with us.

When we reach out to a wayward child only to be rebuffed again, He is with us.

When we accept a calling that is out of our comfort zone, He is with us.

When we set healthy boundaries that might upset some around us, He is with us.

When we sacrifice to serve Him, He is with us.

He is with us when we choose to feel love in the form of grief, when we care for our aging parents, when we give our children second and third and a thousandth chance. He is with us when we struggle to overcome addiction, change jobs, move across the country, or kneel down to repent.

He is with us when we walk into the room of a dying loved one to say goodbye for the first, the second, and even the third time.

When we choose to walk into the pain to get to something better, God is with us.

He is with you.

And not only is He with you, but He will help your suffering have a purpose.

The Savior Himself says:

> If thou are called to pass through tribulation; if thou art in perils among false brethren; if thou art in perils among robbers; if thou art in perils by land or by sea;
>
> If thou art accused with all manner of false accusations; if thine enemies fall upon thee; if they tear thee from the society of thy father and mother and brethren and sisters; and if with a drawn sword thine enemies tear thee from the bosom of thy wife, and of thine offspring, and thine elder son, although but six years of age, shall cling to thy garments, and shall say, My father, my father, why can't you stay with us? O, my father, what are the men going to do with you? and if then he shall be thrust from thee by the sword, and thou be dragged to prison, and thine enemies prowl around thee like wolves for the blood of the lamb;

And if thou shouldst be cast into the pit, or into the hands of murderers, and the sentence of death passed upon thee; if thou be cast into the deep; if the billowing surge conspire against thee; if fierce winds become thine enemy; if the heavens gather blackness, and all the elements combine to hedge up the way; and above all, if the very jaws of hell shall gape open the mouth wide after thee, know thou, my son, that all these things shall give thee experience, and shall be for thy good. (Doctrine and Covenants 122:5–7)

There is power in choosing to walk into holy places—even ones that are painful. Some things can only be accessed through suffering, like the Atonement of Jesus Christ. And there are some tender mercies that can only by accessed through suffering, like empathy, growth, understanding, and love.

Looking back at my three goodbyes, I realize that Mom only said goodbye once—on that last visit. It's as if she knew what took me three times to understand. No matter how many goodbyes we say, there will always be another hello. I will see her again.

This is the beauty of eternal perspective and "thinking celestial."[15] The pain we feel now is but for a heavenly moment. The Savior left the garden, was taken off the cross, and rose in glory and immortality three days later.

As we invite Heavenly Father and Jesus Christ into our suffering with us, we can be assured that the relationship we have with Them and the blessings that come from Their presence and power will outlive all our pain.

Just as grief connects me to my mom now in heaven, I've learned that suffering can connect me to my Father in Heaven and my Savior. Whether it's thrust upon us, or we choose to walk into it for a greater why, we can find help and grace in our pain. We can find purpose in our pain. We can find hope, strength, and love. We can find Them. And I know that when I return to Them, I will see Mom again, and I won't ever have to say goodbye again.

---

15. See Russell M. Nelson, *Think Celestial!*, General Conference (Salt Lake City, UT), Oct 2023, Gospel Library App.

VIII

THE RACE OF LIFE

By Elaine S. Dalton

"Wherefore, ye must press forward with a steadfastness in Christ, having a perfect brightness of hope, and a love of God and of all men. Wherefore, if ye shall press forward, feasting upon the word of Christ, and endure to the end, behold, thus saith the Father: Ye shall have eternal life." —2 Nephi 31:20

EARLY ONE BEAUTIFUL SPRING MORNING, MY HUSBAND, STEVE, AND I decided to go for a run together. That was a rare agreement for a couple of reasons. First, Steve is a seasoned runner, and second, I'm competitive. That combination does not usually create a pleasant bonding experience. We each recognized this, and so we rarely ran or trained together. However, I was feeling rested and great that morning, needed someone to push me, and thought I could keep up with him. Steve also promised that he would "go slow" for me.

The run started out pleasantly together, and I became more confident. However, as Steve warmed up and found his pace, it became more and more difficult for me to keep up with him. Nevertheless, I pushed forward, remembering that there was a long steep hill ahead in a couple of miles and that I was able to run hills easier than Steve.

As we approached the hill, I smiled. I knew this was where I could outrun him. But to my dismay, Steve ran as if we were on flat ground! His pace quickened and he quickly surged ahead of me. He was running at his best that morning and I quickly fell behind—way behind.

My pride got the best of me and I decided to turn around—to quit competing because I knew I couldn't keep up. Not to be outdone, I called ahead to Steve, "I'm quitting! I'm turning around now, and I'll meet you back at the car." Then I quickly turned around and started to run downhill and breathe a little easier. I hadn't gone far, however, when I felt a strong hand on my shoulder. It was Steve. He took my hand, turned me around, and proceeded to say something I will never forget. "Elaine," he said, "haven't you learned that you never quit or turn back when you're in the middle of a hill?" Then he took my hand and we together, side by side, ran to the top of the hill. Somehow ascending the hill became much easier for me with my hand in his. When we arrived at the top, it was there that I realized that I if I had quit and just gone back to the car, I would have missed the most glorious sunrise. The light was spread over the entire valley below. The site was breathtaking.

It was there on that hill, in that moment, that I was grateful for my husband's wise counsel. I realized that if I had turned around and quit, I would have missed a life-changing glorious experience shared with my husband.

It was Nephi who exhorted each of us to "press forward with a perfect brightness of hope, and a love of God and of all men." I learned that morning that I *could* "press forward," relying on my past training and the strength of my husband. I also learned a life-altering lesson: "Never make a decision to quit or turn back when you're in the middle of a hill."

Some of you may feel that you're currently on a hill, so to speak, because of your life experiences—whatever they may be. You may feel that you can't keep going—that you need to quit or turn back and find your comfort zone. But that's not why we came to earth. We came to continue to make choices, to overcome opposition, to continue to progress, and to press forward through trials, challenges, doubts, and temptations. I have learned that we only progress when we are moved out of our comfort zones.

Paul taught, "Wherefore seeing we also are compassed about with so great a cloud of witnesses, let us lay aside every weight, and the sin which doth so easily beset us, and let us run with patience the race that is set before us, Looking unto Jesus the author and finisher of our faith; who for the joy that was set before him endured the cross" (Hebrews 12:1–2).

God has a race for each of us to run. God has a purpose for our lives. There will be difficult challenges, but there will also be great opportunities if we endure. To run this race means to acknowledge that God's purpose for our lives is what matters, and to make it our number one priority to discover and fulfill this purpose.

Each of you is uniquely qualified to run your own race, and God will lead you along. He will be "on your right hand and on your left," and His "angels [will be] round about you, to bear you up" (Doctrine and Covenants 84:88) as you do so. Why? Because we have entered into a covenant relationship with Him and His Beloved Son. When we renew and keep our covenants, we all can have the absolute assurance that we are not walking or running this race of earth life alone. He is tethered to us.

He has promised, "Come unto me, and all who labor and are heavy laden, and I will give you rest. Take my yoke upon you, learn of me: for I am meek and lowly in heart. And you will find rest for your souls. For my yoke is easy, and my burden is light" (Matthew 11:28–30).

Consider substituting the word *covenants* in this scripture for the word *yoke* so it reads, "My covenants are easy, and my burden is light."

That is an absolute truth because we have made covenants with Him and renew them each week as we partake of the sacrament. As we "always remember Him," He will always remember us. Always! He will enable us. We can view the challenges in our lives as catalysts for change. And we can do it because we are yoked with the Savior. We move through this life shoulder to shoulder with the One who has taken upon Himself all of our pains, sorrows, infirmities, weaknesses, and sickness (see Alma 7:11). He knows how to "succor" us, a word which means "to run to." He will run to us and always be with us!

On another run, in that same canyon, I learned another life-altering lesson. I was running early in the morning with a group of friends.

It was the morning before Thanksgiving, and as we ran, we called out things we were grateful for. I was filled with gratitude for so many things. Our son had just returned from a successful mission, and our entire family was going to be together for the first time in over two years.

When it came time for me to share, I happily shouted out, "I'm grateful for a strong, healthy body!" And then, all of a sudden, I found myself flat on the ground, having slipped on black ice. As I tried to stand up, pain surged through my body, and I realized that my leg was badly broken just above my ankle. I asked my friends to run for help and to call my husband and tell him to come as fast as he could. As they ran down the canyon, I laid in the road alone, crying and praying and hoping to stay positive and not go into shock. But I was shivering and could feel it coming.

Suddenly I saw light in the distance. It was the headlights of a car in the distance, and they were coming straight toward me! I thought at one point that it was Steve coming to rescue me, but then I realized it was not and that I was going to be run over by that car! All I could do was pray. Thankfully, the driver saw me, slammed on his brakes, and came to a quick stop. He jumped out of his car and said, "I'm so glad I stopped. I thought you were a garbage bag in the road." (I certainly felt like one!)

I told him what had happened and that my leg was broken badly, and then I asked him if he happened to be a member of The Church of Jesus Christ of Latter-day Saints. He looked down and softly said, "Yes." I asked him if he could give me a blessing so that I could endure the pain and not go into shock until help came. He hesitated. Then he said, "No, I can't. You better wait for your husband to do that." Then he turned around, got in his car, and drove away, leaving me lying in the road.

I can't remember the details of the ride to the hospital or anything that happened thereafter, except that my husband came and put me in the back of the car, and my friend rode with us singing "I Know That My Redeemer Lives." And in the car, on that ride, I knew He did. Then everything became a blur.

I remember the curtains of the cubicle in the emergency room opening, and I saw my husband and each of our five sons. They had come to give me a blessing. I was so grateful that morning for those five big young men, for the priesthood power they honored, and for the blessing that was given by my righteous husband and our precious sons. The pain stopped.

My mind went back to the day that President Gordon B. Hinckley performed our sealing in the Salt Lake Temple. At that time, he gave Steve and me some advice, telling us something that neither of us will ever forget. He advised us "to always live your lives such that when you are in need of a blessing, you can approach the Father out of righteousness rather than mercy, and He will bless you."

That morning in the emergency room of the hospital, it was crystal clear that his advice about striving to remain worthy was extremely important. And every temptation avoided and sin repented of was indeed very worth it!

Spiritual perseverance allows us to develop faith in Jesus Christ, to come to know Him, to see and acknowledge His hand in our lives, and to walk with Him. Even though our journey may not be easy, I believe that as we stay close to the Lord, repent, keep our covenants, never give up, and learn how to access the redeeming and enabling power of the Savior's infinite Atonement, we will be given the needed strength to keep pressing forward, yoked with the Savior through our covenants. With His help, we will be able to run our own unique race on the covenant path. Then, when all is done, each of us will proclaim, as did Paul, "I have fought the good fight. I have finished the race. I have kept the faith" (2 Timothy 4:7 New International Version).

Whether it's a hill run that we feel like we're losing, a healthy body that breaks a leg, or honoring covenants and serving faithfully, the Lord will sustain us and enable us to work through everything so that we can help those in need, recover in a warm hospital, and see the sunrise over the hill crests. The hills we face may be steep, but the sunrises await us at the top. And Christ will help us get there.

IX

HE MEETS US WHERE WE ARE

By Kimberly DowDell

It was October 3, 2010. I was pregnant with my fourth child and had been in labor all day. My husband was in Chicago undergoing training for a new job, but thankfully, my sister happened to be in town for the St. George Utah Marathon that weekend.

After several hours of denying I was in labor, I couldn't put off the inevitable any longer, and my sister excitedly drove me to the hospital. I say "excited" because she was a mother of three and had only experienced giving birth, not watching it. To say she was absolutely thrilled to be the one *watching* the birth was an understatement. She was determined to be the best birthing cheerleader I ever had!

Knowing my husband would be gone, we hoped that I wouldn't go into labor and out son could wait for the induction scheduled after his return. Instead, I went into labor early. As the contractions began early that Sunday morning, I refused to believe I was in labor because I didn't want to deliver the baby without my husband, the one I needed most! When we arrived at the hospital, I was dilated to six centimeters and knew there was no turning back.

Within a couple of hours, our sweet baby Jack arrived. He had the sweetest, most beautiful little face. At first glance, I thought something was different, but I couldn't put my finger on it. Everyone around me was talking in hushed tones, and I sensed something was wrong. As the nurse examined him, the doctor asked, "Is there a heart murmur?" She said no and I thought, "Heart murmur?" Everyone around me kept asking me if he looked like any of my other children, and I thought, "No, I don't think he looks anything like any of my other children," but I couldn't put my finger on why that was.

Labor and delivery were exhausting, and once the nurses and doctor left the room, I found myself trying to relax but couldn't. I knew deep down that something wasn't right. My husband had experienced the birth via cell phone, and as far as he was concerned, everything was okay. Within a couple of hours after delivery, the pediatrician arrived. It was late at night, and I thought, "Wow, this pediatrician is really on top of things!" He stood across the room from me and abruptly exclaimed, "We think the baby has Down syndrome." I was so shocked; I couldn't get any words out of my mouth.

I was so glad my sister was there. I don't believe there are any coincidences in life, and looking back at this experience, I can see Heavenly Father guiding me through it. In fact, President Thomas S. Monson once said, "There is a guiding hand above all things. Often when things happen, it's not by accident. One day when we look back at the seeming coincidences of our lives, we will realize that perhaps they weren't so coincidental after all." With this in mind, Heavenly Father knew I would need her wisdom, her love, and her ability to feel exactly what I was feeling in that moment. I looked at my sister standing beside my bed with tears in my eyes as she confidently said, "It doesn't matter!" Those were the exact words I needed to hear and the strength I needed to feel.

Growing up, I hadn't had much interaction with people who had Down syndrome. In fact, my husband recently asked me, "Where did your mind go when you were told that Jack had Down syndrome? What did you envision his life would look like that made you so worried?"

To be honest, when it comes to explaining the flood of emotions that hit you after receiving such unexpected news is like trying to catch lightning in a bottle. Looking back on those thoughts, feelings, and emotions is like flipping through an old photo album—each picture brings back a flood of memories. For those who haven't been in this situation, understanding without experiencing it firsthand is like trying to explain the taste of chocolate to someone who's never had it. These reflections capture exactly what I went through in those first moments and hours after Jack's birth. I'm sharing them in the hope that they might offer some comfort to others who find themselves in a similar place.

Suddenly, the baby I had been picturing in my mind shifted. His life would follow an alternate path than the one I had planned and hoped it would be. His future felt more uncertain than it had with his older siblings and was accompanied by tests and diagnoses that I had never heard of or knew anything about. I had all these worries buzzing around in my head—would he walk, talk, read, or get to enjoy sports? Would he have friends or be made fun of? Would he find love like everyone else and get married? Now, looking back, I can see Heavenly Father had placed individuals in my path who were optimistic and hopeful for his future, but in those moments I still couldn't help but feel a little sad and grieve for the loss of the baby I thought I was having. It was overwhelming, and I needed time to grieve and process my emotions.

However, shortly after birth, other concerns with Jack's health began to arise, and we became very concerned with problems he was having because he was unable to keep food down and was constantly lethargic.

Due to a series of events, two weeks following Jack's birth, he became very ill and was barely holding on to life. We fasted as a family, and Jack received a priesthood blessing. To this day, I know Jack is here with us because of that blessing and fast. Soon after, he was transported to Primary Children's Hospital where he was treated for duodenal atresia, a condition where your stomach isn't attached to your intestines. I spent two months alone in the hospital with Jack while my husband finished up his training in Chicago and our older children were in Cedar City with their grandparents. It was a very trying time as I was living in the hospital alone, completely in survival mode.

As I watched the seasons change through the hospital windows, I remember praying to Heavenly Father, saying, "I can't do this!" And in my mind, I immediately received an affirming answer: "You *are* doing it!" Heavenly Father frequently sent angels to minister to me on His behalf. These earthy angels brought food, much-needed conversation, friendship, arms to embrace me in a hug, shoulders to cry on, and loved ones to carry this very heavy burden with me.

Although I had many visitors, some of my hardest moments were spent alone watching Jack suffer through frequent blood draws, IV changes, PICC line insertions, surgeries, and so on. As a parent, watching your child suffer and experience pain is one of the most mentally and emotionally challenging experiences in life. What I wouldn't have done to take that pain away from him.

After spending what felt like two years in the hospital, Jack was finally discharged and we were reunited as a family. Despite the numerous tender mercies and answered prayers during those months, life at home felt different.

After the dust settled and we finally returned home, a wave of depression washed over me. The sheer exhaustion from those relentless two months in the hospital combined with the overwhelming stress had taken its toll. My mind was cluttered with self-doubt, anxiety, and the daunting task of raising a child with special needs. The weight of inadequacy pressed down on me heavily. Even amidst the comfort of home, occasional worries about Jack's future crept in, and I found myself longing for a sign from above, a glimpse from Heavenly Father to assure me that everything would eventually fall into place and be okay.

I didn't realize it at the time, but I was severely depressed! Those days were dark and were spent in agony. I wanted to sleep but couldn't. My mind constantly triggered with worry, guilt, and shame for not feeling like I was enough. How was I going to do this?! I didn't want to live. It was then that Heavenly Father intervened. I was out driving one day and out of the blue received a phone call from my sweet sister-in-law, who happens to be a life coach. When I answered the phone, she said, "I don't know why, but the Spirit has been nagging me all day that I need to call you. What's going on?"

Heavenly Father had sent an angel, and it was a miraculous tender mercy. I told her all of the things I was feeling that I didn't dare say to anyone out loud. She listened, she validated, and she helped me get to a place where I was ready to heal. From that moment, I let everything go.

Throughout this time, I failed to realize that the Savior felt and endured every ounce of pain I was going through. His Atonement wasn't only for the mistakes I had made in life but for this kind of pain as well. From the shock of an unexpected diagnosis and the accompanying grief, to the heartache, pain, worry, and loneliness in the hospital, and even in the moments of sorrow and feelings of inadequacy, He felt and experienced it all for *me*!

Once I realized He had been patiently waiting with open arms to comfort and carry my pain and grief, my feelings of sorrow and depression began to lift. Through this experience, I have learned to turn to Jesus in life's storms; He is always there to help and bring comfort. This transformation did not happen overnight, and it took a lot of effort on my part, but I've learned I don't have to face trials alone. The Atonement is ongoing because the Savior is always reaching out to heal and guide us. There is no trial too big or too small. His love is unconditional, and we are worth it!

One of my favorite stories is of the woman at the well. This story really hits home for me because it has made me think about my own journey and where the Savior has shown up for me in my life. This woman wasn't attending the temple or a church meeting; the Savior found her doing a simple chore—getting water from the well. As I've thought about this, I've learned to recognize where He tends to shows up for me in my life. It happens most often through people and experiences, and even the most simple place—the gym.

One standout experience is when He nudged me back into teaching fitness classes. Can you imagine the group fitness room, during a Zumba class, becoming my place of peace and renewal? It might sound cheesy, but those workout spaces were where I found real healing through Jesus. Dancing became the one thing I could do to let go of all the heavy stuff I was experiencing. In that special space, I felt a close connection with Him. It was as if Heavenly Father had set it all up to assist me through my healing process.

Thinking back on it, I've realized that these divine moments don't always happen in fancy places. Sometimes it's the regular, day-to-day stuff where the Savior decides to show up. Just like the woman at the well, I've discovered that the Savior meets me in unexpected places, turning normal, everyday parts of life into chances for connection and healing. Where or when He shows up in our lives isn't a coincidence. It always happens at the perfect moment, exactly when we need it most.

Elder Neal A. Maxwell said, "The same God that placed that star in a precise orbit millennia before it appeared over Bethlehem, in celebration of the birth of the Babe, has given at least equal attention to the placement of each of us in precise human orbits so that we may, if we will, illuminate the landscape of our individual lives, so that our light may not only lead others but warm them as well."[16]

Heavenly Father knows us, He is aware of us, and He is placing people and experiences into our lives that will bring us joy.

I am here to tell you there is joy beyond grief, beyond pain and suffering, beyond those unexpected circumstances in life that turn your entire world upside down and leave you feeling unsure of life and your ability to feel happiness and experience joy.

As I started to heal, I told you of the glimpse of my son's future life that I had hoped for and prayed that Heavenly Father would give to me. Well, one day, my husband and I stumbled across a video on YouTube of a young man in high school with Down syndrome sharing his daily routine on the internet. He independently rode his bike to the YMCA to swim every day, made his own smoothie for breakfast, and had a system for organizing his day that helped him remember what his to-do tasks were that needed to be done. To us, as parents of a baby with Down syndrome, we were amazed and thought his life and personality were extraordinary! It was no coincidence that Heavenly Father led us to this video—it was the happy glimpse into Jack's future that we needed to see!

---

16. Neal A. Maxwell, *That My Family Should Partake* (Salt Lake City, UT: Deseret Book, 1974), 86.

Over the years, we've talked about this video and how it gave us so much hope for Jack's future and brought much-needed comfort into our lives.

Today Heavenly Father has blessed me with the gift of sharing our life and Jack with the world on social media. Our Instagram, TikTok, and YouTube took off when we started sharing the sweet bond between Jack and his family members. Followers frequently comment on Jack's infectious smile and uplifting personality. His joy radiates through his entire being, bringing happiness to others daily. Jack is truly one of a kind, and followers often express gratitude for letting them share in his journey. Jack's positive outlook encourages people to appreciate life's little moments, and we often hear, "If only we all could take a page out of Jack's book." Without even realizing it, he spreads the Savior's light, sharing good news along the way and helping others feel Him in their lives daily. Through our social media channels, my hope is for Jack's life to offer a glimpse of peace and comfort to those facing their own diagnosis or health challenges.

Through these experiences, I've learned to recognize the importance of drawing closer to the Savior and have developed a stronger desire to spread happiness, peace, and positivity. I've come to realize that Christ doesn't demand perfection. The Savior, through His Atonement, makes up the difference in all areas of our lives: pain, inadequacy, sorrow, sin, grief—He felt it *all*! And all He requires is for us to have faith in Him, trust in Him, and give our best effort each day.

One of my favorite practices is to seek out divine moments when the Savior shows up in my life. Whether I'm folding laundry, at the gym, cuddling with Jack during story time, or even in the quiet moments of a shower, I find Him there. The Savior unfailingly appears and bridges the gap when needed. When I take time to identify these moments, I am reminded of His continual influence, love, and daily encouragement in my life that provides me with feelings of reassurance and peace, especially when facing trials.

Life, although challenging at times, is truly amazing. While our individual experiences differ, we've all faced difficulty in one way or another or supported someone through their own individual struggles. My challenge to you is to seek a closer connection to the Savior and invite His help in all ways possible. Take time to recognize His daily presence in your life and where He shows up for you. Pray regularly for guidance and you will receive it. The Savior wants so badly for us to know Him and is often working through other people and our experiences to make this happen.

X
Two Truths
By William G. Perez

Both Things Are True

As a missionary on the Texas-Mexico border, I learned the valuable adage "¡si no pica, no es rica!" In other words, "if it's not spicy, it's not tasty!" Have you ever eaten something that was intensely hot but still delicious? At least for some of us, the teary eyes and stinging taste buds are totally worth the mouthwatering moment. In fact, they are part of the experience. Though I recognize that fiery foods are not for everyone, I believe that "¡si no pica, no es rica!" can be a metaphor for our individual and collective journeys. The tangled and tragic parts of our lives—the spicy, sour, or bitter moments—are part of a larger recipe that culminates in a dish— a life, or a history—that "is most precious" and that is "sweet above all that is sweet" (Alma 32:42). Surely, it will all be worth it. Even Adam and Eve came to see that their fall was actually a catalyst for their joy and redemption (see Moses 5:10-11). But how can something so intense ever be appetizing? How can spicy and sweet, darkness and light, the all that precedes the worth it, be integral parts of mortality's menu without canceling each other out? Despite the desire of catering only to our sweet tooths, learning to embrace the smorgasbord of savors along the way is a taste worth acquiring. I have found that only in embracing all of life's ingredients together, accepting their coexistence, and being comfortable in a space where each has merit, can we find wholeness.

This allowance of seeming contradictions in a search for authentic reality has become very meaningful in my personal pursuit of happiness and holiness.[17] I did not feel that I had the conceptual framework to adequately express it until I stumbled across the title of a book by Latter-day Saint historian Kate Holbrook. Before even reading her collection of essays entitled *Both Things Are True*, I knew that this was exactly what I had been trying to explain in my own life. Expanding Joseph Smith's observation that "by proving contraries, truth is made manifest,"[18] Holbrook "shows how a covenant life can be lived in the open space between contrary ideas that are equally valid but independently incomplete."[19] As she wrestles through tensions such as a true and living church, or revelation being both divine and human, or the conflicting injunctions to forget and remember, Holbrook reminds readers that it is okay to inhabit spaces in which both things are true. Contrary to common assumptions, ugly truths don't cancel out pretty ones, and spicy foods can be part of sweet meals. This insight has taken mental, emotional, and spiritual weight off my shoulders. It helps me appreciate the all in "it will all be worth it." By "all" I mean those sometimes spicy, sour, or bitter morsels that are a needful part of the succulent banquet prepared for us by loving heavenly parents. Incidentally, this appreciation for complementary contraries didn't sink deep into my heart through physical suffering and healing, or through grappling with tribulation alongside God's promises of redemption. It occurred as I confronted Latter-day Saint church history.

---

17. See Dieter F. Uchtdorf, *Of Regrets and Resolutions*, General Conference (Salt Lake City UT), October 2012, Gospel Library App.
18. Letter to Israel Daniel Rupp, 5 June 1844, 1, josephsmithpapers.org.
19. Kate Holbrook, *Both Things Are True* (Salt Lake City, UT: Deseret Book, 2023), xiii.

From the Seminary to the Academy

I had been a religious educator in the seminaries and institutes program of The Church of Jesus Christ of Latter-day Saints for just over seven years—most of my adult life at that point. I considered myself converted to the restored gospel and gladly immersed in the faith of my fathers. I loved how I had come to find Christ through "Mormonism."[20] I also found peace in temple worship and church service. As part of my profession, I was constantly surrounded by faithful colleagues. I was immersed day in and day out in the business of teaching the gospel of Jesus Christ as found in the words of ancient and modern prophets, with the goal of bringing students into the fold and retaining them. It was literally my job to defend the kingdom and to portray doctrines and history in the most positive and faith-promoting light possible. This commission came with its unique set of burdens. Still, I carried them joyfully.

During this time, I also completed a master's degree at Brigham Young University in religious education. Although the program was narrow in scope, it helped me to think critically about my faith in ways I never had before. I learned about groundbreaking shifts in Latter-day Saint history, about resources and archives still up for grabs, and about classic stories and characters that were more nuanced than I had ever considered. This experience lit a fire in me for continued scholarship, both spiritual and secular. In 2021, I made the difficult decision to leave church employment and pursue a doctorate degree in American religious history at Florida State University.

The transition was bittersweet (both can be part of the same meal, right?). When I finally began my much anticipated first semester as a PhD student, it seemed as though I lived an entire life of study in the first two days. I summarized day one to my wife with the word "inspiring." Day two was summarized with the word "discouraging."

---

20. I use the term *Mormon* here and in subsequent sections to better technically encapsulate the historical and academic world in which I became immersed. In this context, *Mormon* is meant "to characterize aspects of the history and cultural traditions that shape the lives of many members of The Church of Jesus Christ of Latter-day Saints but that are not formal parts of the institutional church." Quincy D. Newell and Benjamin E. Park, "Multiplicity: An Editors' Introduction," *Mormon Studies Review* 7 (2020): 4.

I described my experience to a friend in a message saying, "I am disoriented and inspired and excited and sickened at the same time." I felt that in this brief introductory period I had already thought more critically about religion and my own faith than ever before. The class discussions were stimulating and terrifying. My mind flooded with ideas of what I might want to consider, research, and write about.

As I walked back to my car after a three-hour seminar, I felt heavy and was pained with a few burning questions: How could religion, something that has brought so much joy and hope to so many, also be the source of so much discomfort and conflict? How am I supposed to talk or write about my faith—the faith that I love and espouse—in ways that might sometimes be construed as negative, unflattering, or even contrary to the cause? Could my testimony of the restored gospel also encompass parts of its history that I wasn't able to satisfactorily explain? I couldn't see a clear path around it all. The very thought of personally producing the type of Mormon history I was interested in filled me with guilt, even heartbreak—the kind of guilt or heartbreak you might feel when speaking ill about or confronting wrongs committed by a cherished family member whom you are expected to side with and defend at all costs. What if after it was all said and done, I didn't even want to believe anymore? I was drowning in the spicy part of the meal.

To this point, when I had to err, I always erred on the side of warm and fuzzy when it came to the Church. But now here I was, surrounded by people who referred to themselves as "recovering Southern Baptists" and "neo-paganists," who wanted to think critically about religion—all religions. I felt free to share my thoughts, concerns, hesitancies, and yes even faith, without being judged or feeling like a heretic. As I gradually picked up on the academic lingo, I learned that, as argued by religious historian Bruce Lincoln, "to practice history of religions in a fashion consistent with the discipline's claim of title is to insist on discussing the temporal, contextual, situated, interested, human, and material dimensions of those discourses, practices, communities, and institutions that characteristically represent themselves as eternal, transcendent, spiritual, and divine."[21] What a conflict of interests! I didn't know if I could do it. I didn't know if I could swim in the deep end. What if I published something that caused someone else to question that which I found to be "eternal, transcendent, spiritual, and divine" within The Church of Jesus Christ of Latter-day Saints? Maybe I just wouldn't even open that can of worms. Would I disappoint my God? My church leaders? My family? Was it an unforgivable betrayal? Maybe I would study something else. Or better yet, maybe I would just quit without dissecting my faith and leave my reputation intact. I felt torn between sweet and sour extremes that I thought couldn't possibly exist on the same plate. In this state of mind, I might have re-written my opening adage to "¡si pica, no puede ser rica!" or "if it's spicy, it cannot be tasty!"

I wrestled with these thoughts all night. I verbalized them to my wife and to the Father in Heaven that I had come to know through Mormonism itself. If He was listening, what would He want me to do? The next morning, I knelt to pray before a brief scripture study. I had decided, at the very least, that I would make it a point to still feast on that which I considered spiritual each day. Immediately, a thought entered my being that instantly resolved my double-mindedness (see James 1:8) and eased my burden. I sat down and chased that thought into 1 Nephi 9 in the Book of Mormon.

Two Sets of Records

The chapter heading reads: "Nephi makes two sets of records—Each is called the plates of Nephi—The larger plates contain a secular history; the smaller ones deal primarily with sacred things" (1 Nephi 9, chapter heading). There it was. Even the great prophet Nephi, who "labored diligently to write, to persuade our children, and also our brethren to believe in Christ" (2 Nephi 25:23), made it a point to record the history of his people. A history that included "the reign of the kings and the wars and contentions of my people" (1 Nephi 9:4). Wars and contentions? Nephi, and succeeding prophet historians in

---

21. Bruce Lincoln, *Gods and Demons, Priests and Scholars: Critical Explorations in the History of Religions* (Chicago: The University of Chicago Press: 2012), 1.

the Book of Mormon did not try to sugarcoat anything, favoring only the proverbial sweetness. They must have seen value in a "warts and all" history and sought to preserve it just as much as they safeguarded the account of "the ministry" (1 Nephi 9:3) and of those things which they deemed "pleasing unto God and unto those who are not of the world" (1 Nephi 6:6). Both types of records were kept. One did not detract from the validity or importance of the other. In fact, they were both made "for a wise purpose" (1 Nephi 9:5), one which Nephi did not fully comprehend at the time.

As these realizations and their implications sank in, my trepidation over diving into Mormon history and writing about it floated away. Like Nephi, I could confidently keep a secular history that would not diminish my sacred history, regardless of what audiences in either camp might think. I could dive into and question the "wars and contentions" without losing the beauty of "the ministry." And if "the Lord [truly] knoweth all things from the beginning" (1 Nephi 9:6), then what did I have to lose anyway? As J. Reuben Clark is said to have stated, "If we have truth, [it] cannot be harmed by investigation. If we have not truth, it ought to be harmed."[22]

My experience in 1 Nephi gave me the confidence to openly pursue my interests in secular history, in the academic study of religion, and to have frank conversations about my faith—and sometimes lack thereof—without second guessing myself or feeling guilty about doing so.[23] In keeping one set of plates, I need not forfeit the other. The Lord did not intend for me to restrict myself to a diet of only spicy

---

22. D. Michael Quinn, *J. Reuben Clark: The Church Years* (Provo, UT: Brigham Young University Press, 1983), 24.

23. Interestingly, President Gordon B. Hinckley counseled religious educators to spend time in both worlds. He said, "It is imperative that we as teachers in the seminary and institute of religion program of the Church read constantly the scriptures and other books related directly to the history, the doctrine, and the practices of the Church. But we ought also to be reading secular history, the great literature that has survived the ages, and the writings of contemporary thinkers and doers. In so doing we will find inspiration to pass on to our students, who will need all the balanced strength they can get as they face the world into which they move." "Four Imperatives for Religious Educators," in *Teaching Seminary Preservice Readings: Religion 370, 471, and 475* (Salt Lake City, UT: The Church of Jesus Christ of Latter-day Saints, 2004), 112.

foods or only sweet treats. Both histories were critical for my learning and growth. I committed to always having something in the pipeline for my sacred history even as I obsessed over researching and writing a secular history. I am grateful that there is ample precedent throughout scripture for keeping a secular, "warts and all" history alongside a "sacred" one. Both things are true! And they do not detract from each other. Together they create a beautiful, well-balanced meal. In cuisine as in life, "¡si no pica, no es rica!" Regardless of the dogmatic clamor of doctors or disciples claiming that only their camp has merit, there is ample room for honoring a variety of experiences. The parts we may not like or understand do not invalidate the parts that surely come from heaven.[24] Allowing for this paradox as it pertains to history has been a saving grace as I continue to "seek learning by study and also by faith" (D&C 109:7).

Messy Mortality and Earthy Golden Plates

Truth be told, taking the sacred and the secular, or the all and the worth it as part of "one eternal round" (1 Nephi 10:19) can be messy. It cuts across neatly-defined dichotomies that push bitter cups toward the back of the refrigerator and only display the sweet drinks. But as I recall, the Savior Jesus Christ did drink a bitter cup. Only then could his wondrous power sweeten our own.[25] One of Jesus' most poignant promises actually sounds very similar to "it will all be worth it." He reminded us that "In the world ye shall have tribulation: but be of good cheer: I have overcome the world" (John 16:33). The Lord did not shy away from the reality of tribulation even as he reiterated its divine conclusion. His statement is hopeful, encouraging, and

---

24. For a great practical example of this concept, see Michael A. Goodman and W. Justin Dyer, "The Family Proclamation: The Secular and Spiritual Context," *Religious Educator* 24, no. 2 (2023): 107–133.

25. The experience of the children of Israel recorded in Exodus 15 provides a beautiful symbol of the Savior. Moses is directed to cast a tree into the bitter and undrinkable waters of Marah to make them sweet (see Exodus 15:22–25). Elder Orson F. Whitney poetically expressed a similar concept when he described the Redeemer of his soul "whose wondrous pow'r hath raised me up and filled with sweet my bitter cup." "Savior, Redeemer of My Soul," *Hymns*, The Church of Jesus Christ of Latter-day Saints, Salt Lake City, UT, no. 112, Gospel Library App.

framed in an eternal perspective. But it still includes an ugly truth: "ye shall have tribulation." Sometimes we are tempted to skirt around ugly truths. We sweep them under the rug and cling to the worth it stuff, the "overcome the world" stuff. Yet the enduring truth is that as much as we would like to deal only with the better halves—the sweet and not the spicy—without both parts together, "all things must have vanished away" (2 Nephi 2:13).

This paradoxical principle dates to our first parents whose fall away from the presence of the Gods made possible an ascent toward them. The Savior's own condescension is a beautiful reminder of the need to experience suffering and infirmity—including the infirmity of loss of faith—as part of a glorious journey of ascension (see D&C 88:6).[26] As President Russell M. Nelson explained, Jesus "taught us that He literally descended beneath all things to rise above all things."[27] Correspondingly, Latter-day Saints believe in a God who rejoices as well as in a God who weeps (see Moses 7:28-29). As Sister Tamara W. Runia expressed, "there are times when earth, our temporal home, feels like an island of sorrow—moments when I have one eye of faith and the other eye is weeping."[28] And yet each eye's vision is valid. Both things can be true. It will *ALL* be worth it.

One final example of seemingly incongruent realities—a spicy and sweet paradox—whose collision is greater than the sum of its parts is that of the golden plates procured by Joseph Smith in 1827. Striking metal sheets, carefully crafted, expertly engraved, containing "the fulness of the everlasting gospel," translated by "the gift and power of God" (D&C 135:3). On the other hand, they are time-worn, buried in the ground, "[sent] forth out of the earth" (Moses 7:62), a record

---

26. President M. Russell Ballard quoted and paraphrased Alma 7:11–12 as follows: "Where will you go to be taught about a Savior who is your best friend, who not only suffered for your sins but who also suffered 'pains and afflictions and temptations of every kind' so 'that his bowels may be filled with mercy, according to the flesh, that he may know according to the flesh how to succor his people according to their infirmities,' including, I believe, the infirmity of loss of faith?" "To Whom Shall We Go?," *Ensign*, Nov. 2016, 91.
27. Russell M. Nelson, "Why This Holy Land?," *Ensign*, Dec. 1989, 15.
28. Tamara W. Runia, "Seeing God's Family through the Overview Lens," *Liahona*, Nov. 2023, 68.

riddled with imperfections (see Moroni 8:12, 9:31-33). Although the plates assert themselves to be written by the spirit of prophecy and of revelation . . . to the convincing of Jew and Gentile that JESUS is the CHRIST" (Title Page of The Book of Mormon), Moroni, their last guardian, expresses a painful awareness of "our weakness in writing" because "of the awkwardness of our hands" (Ether 12:23-24). Even though they were delivered to him by an angel, Joseph Smith still had to hide the sacred treasure in a log, "under the hearth, beneath the floor of his father's house, and in piles of grain."[29] Do the more mundane (spicy) aspects of the golden plates negate their divine (sweet) characteristics? Does their all make them not worth it?

In his book, *A Secular Age*, Charles Taylor argues that since the 1500s, society has increasingly transitioned from living within a cosmos of enchantment, one where the supernatural played an active role in everyday affairs, to one of disenchantment, where buffered selves have erected a boundary that shuts out the spiritual.[30] For those who embrace a disenchanted world, the transcendent and the immanent cannot coexist. For them, both things cannot be true. We can either have divine golden plates or elusive, man-made records. That sounds like a very dull diet. On the other hand, the restored gospel necessitates enchantment. It enables a life fully lived in the "dark and dreary wilderness" of mortality (1 Nephi 8:4) while still experiencing "the tender mercies of the Lord" (1 Nephi 1:20). The covenant path does not confine us to an either-or paradigm. Instead, it empowers us in savoring the wide range of experiences needful for our eternal development. Sacred scripture reminds us that "if [we] never should have bitter [we] could not know the sweet" (D&C 29:39). By embracing the doctrine of Christ, we can have hope in the divine enchantment that surrounds us and awaits us, even as we deal with life's more mundane disenchantments.

---

29. *Saints: The Story of the Church of Jesus Christ in the Latter Days*, vol. 1, *The Standard of Truth, 1815–1846* (Salt Lake City: The Church of Jesus Christ of Latter-day Saints, 2018), 38, 43.
30. See Charles Taylor, *A Secular Age* (Cambridge, MA: The Belknap Press of Harvard University, 2007), chapter 1.

To this end, consider what Latter-day Saint historian Richard Bushman observed about the golden plates in his book, *Joseph Smith's Gold Plates: A Cultural History*:

> As [Joseph Smith's] account made clear, the plates were both of the earth and of heaven. They were mundane, material, historical on the one hand, and divine, mysterious, holy, on the other. They moved back and forth across the line that divided the natural and the supernatural.... When a few of Smith's friends were allowed to view the plates, their testimonies again broke down into heavenly and mundane versions. Three of them said that "an angel of God came down from heaven" to lay the plates before them, and the voice of God proclaimed that they "have been translated by the gift and power of God." The remaining eight experienced nothing like the first three. There was no heavenly presence, no angel, no voice from heaven. The eight witnesses said only that they had "seen and hefted the plates." The angel turned the pages of the plates for the three witnesses; the eight witnesses turned the pages for themselves.
>
> Some Latter-day Saints lament that the plates did not remain in Smith's possession as proof he was not making everything up. But that would have broken the spell. The tension between earthly and heavenly would have ended. The plates would have fallen into the hands of archaeologists, historians, and metallurgists and become solely an earthly artifact. In returning to the angel who guarded them, the plates retained their hybrid nature, material and spiritual, their mystery preserved.[31]

It is this "tension between earthly and heavenly" that allows us to accept an enchanted world where falls are deemed fortunate[32] and prophets can be fallible. I used to turn my nose up at the "material" testimony of the eight witnesses, having been taught somewhere along the line that the "spiritual" testimony of the three witnesses was far superior. However, while I acknowledge that only "by the power of the Holy Ghost [we] may know the truth of all things" (Moroni 10:5), I have come to appreciate the value of *both* types of testimonies,

---

31. Richard Bushman, *Joseph Smith's Gold Plates: A Cultural History* (New York: Oxford University Press, 2023), 4–5.
32. See Jeffrey R. Holland, "Where Justice, Love, and Mercy Meet," *Ensign*, May 2015, 105.

two unique flavors working together to provide a clearer view of the mysteries of godliness operating within the reality of my lived experience. As Paul testified, we have been given "treasure in *earthen* vessels, that the excellency of the power may be of God and not of us" (2 Corinthians 4:7; emphasis added).

Jesus Christ Makes It All Worth It

What does this all mean for Latter-day Saint church history in general? What does it mean for imperfect lives and imperfect people? How might this perspective help us to reconcile the "golden" parts with the "buried in the dirt" parts? Taken together, the complete story brings us even closer to "the author and finisher of [our] faith" (Moroni 6:4). As BYU professor Brad Wilcox famously stated, "Jesus doesn't make up the difference. Jesus makes all the difference."[33] This might be especially true when life serves us meals that feel more torturous on the taste buds than pleasing on the palate. As we reflect on unpleasant parts of our collective history, recognize discouraging shortcomings in our own selves, or simply struggle through "the heart-wrenching maze of our mortal experiences"[34]—the all before the worth it—we can remember that the Savior's atoning power encompasses these truths too. His Spirit "speaketh truth and lieth not." He is the bridge between "things as they really are, and of things as they really will be," which "things are manifested unto us plainly, for the salvation of our souls" (Jacob 4:13). Sometimes, as they really are, things can start to taste a little hot. But remember that in the grand scheme of things, "¡si no pica, no es rica!"

Our Redeemer is the God who heals immediately, even though we have been afflicted for 38 years (see John 5:5-9). He is "the man of sorrows" (Isaiah 53:3) who found joy even as he endured the cross (see Hebrews 12:2). His is a mission of condescension and of ascension.[35] Because of Him, we do not have to shy away from disagreeable truths

---

33. Bradley R. Wilcox, "His Grace Is Sufficient" (Brigham Young University devotional, July 12, 2011), 1, speeches.byu.edu.
34. Russell M. Nelson, "Hear Him," *Ensign*, May 2020, 90.
35. See Emily Belle Freeman, "Walking in Covenant Relationship with Christ," *Liahona*, Nov. 2023, 76–79.

out of fear that they invalidate celestial ones. We can be honest and vulnerable as we allow two things to be true at once, trusting that "the truth shall make [us] free" (John 8:32). And "If the Son therefore shall make [us] free, [we] shall be free indeed" (John 8:36). We more fully come to know Him through the natural tensions in which our hearts are filled while our souls are stretched wide. Life's spiciness need not nullify its present and future sweetness. Because both things can be true, I don't need to be defensive or downcast about my church's very human history. Because both things can be true, I don't need to lose hope when encountering catastrophe along the covenant path. And because both things can be true, I know that it will all be worth it.

XI
IT WILL ALL BE WORTH IT

By Fiona Smith

My father once told me that the way of the Faithful is committing to pay the price... even if the cost cannot be known. And trusting that, in the end, it will be worth it.

–J. D. Payne and Patrick McKay
(The Lord of the Rings: The Rings of Power)

IT WAS 1979, A YEAR AFTER THE GLOBAL BAN PREVENTING FULL PARticipation of Church members with African ancestry in priesthood office and temple ordinances ended in The Church of Jesus Christ of Latter-day Saints. Now, inclusively, as when the Church was restored in the 1800s, all worthy men – regardless of race – could hold and administer the ordinances of salvation as priesthood holders, and worthy men and women could enter the temple to worship without restrictions.

American "Mormon" missionaries, as they were typically called then, came to my rough, concrete neighborhood in London, looking like two white CIA agents with smiles. They introduced themselves to my Afro-Caribbean British family of seven and carried a gospel message of how families could be together forever. Family feuds in our household were fairly harmless, so that message held some appeal. The missionaries called us the "golden family" because of our firm acceptance of the faith that asserted itself as the restored early Christian church of Christ. We liked the warm, fuzzy feeling that came with the missionaries and were baptized into the Church that same year.

Under the motto: "Every member a missionary," our home was often crammed with people from our neighborhood of diverse nationalities and backgrounds, who came to listen to the missionaries and watch Church films depicting Americans in large houses with American accents, living American lives. Juxtaposing church films and images against my London inner-city neighborhood, I imagined films showing religious conversions negotiated in all its varieties. Many of the films we saw were made at the church-owned Brigham Young University (BYU) in Utah, America, not too far from where the cinematic headquarters of the Church resided. Intrigued by the idea of pursuing a career with the Church's film department, I applied to BYU and was accepted into a master's program in 1999.

The year previous, in 1998, I had gone on what I intended to be a scouting vacation. I wanted to visit BYU before I put in my application. However, on the plane from London to the US, I had forgotten to fill in my green boarding pass on the plane. That was how I caught an officer's attention. She was very nice and waited for me to fill it out before I proceeded to one of the passport counters. There were four desks ahead, and she directed me to go to one in particular, telling me he'd treat me "good." He was the only black officer there, and I wondered if she implied that I should take that as being in my favor. The immigration officer at the assigned counter asked me why I was in America–a standard question–yet I somehow figured he couldn't simply be asking me about my vacation. He seemed to want to know more about me, that "good" man. So, I told him of my lofty goals and aspirations. I told him that I was going to visit a university in Utah and consider the possibility of studying there in the future. I also shared that I really wanted to develop my talents and hoped to be able to work in my field one day.

I probably expected some praise for my aspirations, a pat on the back, and to be wished good luck. But that didn't happen. I was sent to interrogation, pure and simple, right from his desk to a back room, where an immigration officer got all red in the face while questioning me and pacing the floor. Naively telling the officer my hopes and dreams for a possible future in America quickly turned to trauma. The words *study* and *work* were like *ham* and *beef* in a company of rottweilers. I was fingerprinted, my suitcase cut open and searched. After they got through suspecting I was an imposter named Margaret, a tearful mug shot was taken, and I was escorted very closely back to the plane by three immigration officers armed with guns, batons, and handcuffs, in case I made a run for it. I was told that I wasn't being deported but that I was being sent back to get my papers in order.

Things can change in our lives at any moment. Being sent back to England from America for mentioning my hopes and dreams on a holiday visa when they felt that I had no business doing so was harsh. I was forced to think seriously about getting a study visa if I wanted to return to America even though when I had been sent back, I was merely exploring the possibility of studying there. Difficulties continued when my bishop was reluctant to sign the BYU application papers. "My daughters haven't been able to get into BYU. What makes *you* think you can go?" he exclaimed in our face-to-face at his church office. One Sunday, a BYU study abroad representative who had received the BYU papers on my behalf accompanied me into the bishop's office He signed my application form in stony silence.

My student visa arrived at what could be called God's eleventh hour timing, a day or two before my flight to Utah. I was late for my plane, but it waited for me. I climbed the stairs from the runway, entered the plane, and the passengers erupted in applause, markedly different from a year before when I had cried all the way back to England. Here I was a year later, crying all the way to America because I knew the time had arrived.

At the Atlanta, Georgia airport from England, black officials shrieked at my passport: "You going to Utah? Oh, man, why are you going to Utah? Don't you know there are no black people in Utah?!"

"There are a lot of Mormons in Utah," laughed his colleague in response.

I was fully aware that there were many Mormons in Utah; after all, I was about to be one of them. However, I said very little to these men by way of explanation since I remembered all too vividly my last trip only a year ago.

It will all be worth it.

When I arrived in Utah, it looked like the two-dimensional images I had seen in Church films back in England. Photographically bright, with large mountains backdropped against tree-lined suburban streets. Though known as "happy valley," I assumed the state must have its own share of problems. To my eyes, on a superficial level, however, it looked like a church movie scene made real. The first conversation I had with the chair of Theatre and Media Arts at BYU, was that there needed to be a play about early black pioneers in the Church. I was shocked by my own words as I didn't know whether black Church members had traveled the plains in the nineteenth century. Nevertheless, the department chair informed me that a play called *I Am Jane*, about Jane Manning James and other Black American pioneers, was in fact being workshopped at BYU. I attended that workshop within days of landing in Utah.

During the winter of March 2000, *I Am Jane* premiered in a chapel in Salt Lake City, Utah. In the play, Jane narrates her journey as the audience watches scenes reenacted. Many of the words in the script are taken directly from Jane's biography. Jane was a young woman with relentless faith who, upon joining The Church of Jesus Christ of Latter-day Saints, endured trials inherent in the traveling expeditions of fellow pioneers immigrating to the Salt Lake Valley, most of whom were white at a time when blacks, in most parts of America, were enslaved. Consistent with these times, Jane experienced "rebuff"[36] as a free Black American. Her trials included being denied rightful boat passage with her family in the 1840s, which resulted in her group of eight having to travel more than eight hundred miles on foot from Buffalo, New York, to Nauvoo, Illinois.

---

36. "My Life Sketch, as dictated to Elizabeth J. D. Roundy" (Wilford Woodruff Papers, Church History Library and Archives).

Jane recounted that their shoes wore out, their feet bloodied the ground, and they "were healed forthwith" through prayer.[37] She continued, "When we arrived at Peoria, Illinois, the authorities threatened to put us in jail to get our free papers, we didn't know at first what he meant for we had never been slaves, but he concluded to let us go."[38] In the play, Jane emerges from the obscurity to which history consigned her and becomes a catalyst for a faithful inquiry into the racial ideologies of America in an expanding international Church.

Before the play started, a white audience member approached me and joked that he came to watch the performance because he didn't think there were enough blacks to put on a play in Utah. There were only a few of us there, but we certainly drew attention. In my journal, I noted that "The chapel was filled to the brim with no seats left in the house . . . among the faces of the audience members were a significant number of people of varied races, shades, and colors. Utah is not a place of apparent physical ethnic diversity, so this was an unusual occasion and sight. I gazed at the audience as they gazed with some anticipation at us."

The play was welcomed by some and shunned by others, seen as a vehicle to explore truth and theology, and a means to break one's faith. It permitted an investigation into history's past and present through Jane and other historical characters, such as Elijah Abel of African, English, and Scottish ancestry, ordained to the priesthood as a Seventy Elder before the racial restrictions. The play's first run wrapped at the Bountiful Regional Centre where I performed in the role of Jane in 2003. I wrote my BYU theatre and media arts master's thesis about my performances in theatre and how the Church progressed spiritually and temporally in Jane's Day. As a part of my research, I discovered that in 1839, within four years of pioneer immigrants arriving in the great city of Nauvoo, Joseph Smith ran for the US presidential office and conducted a political campaign to protect the civil rights of members of The Church of Jesus Christ of Latter-day Saints as a minority people. He also spoke out for the rights of the black minority, some of whom were members of the Church. The platform was essentially a

---

37. "My Life Sketch."
38. "My Life Sketch."

secular declaration that, among other topics, condemned slavery, and the poor treatment of blacks. Joseph stated:

> When I viewed the condition of men throughout the world, and more especially in this boasted realm. where the Declaration of Independence . . . holds these truths to be self-evident: that all men are created equal: that they are endowed by their Creator with certain unalienable rights: that among them are life, liberty and the pursuit of happiness, but at the same time, some two or three millions of people are held as slaves for life, because the spirit in them is covered with darker skin than ours. The wisdom which ought to characterize the freest, wisest and most noble nation of the nineteenth century. should, like the sun in his meridian splendor warm every object beneath its rays: and the main efforts . . . ought to be directed to ameliorate the condition of all: black, or white bond or free: for the best of books says. "God hath made of one blood all the nations of men for to dwell on the face of the earth."
>
> Our common country presents to all men the same advantages: the same facilities; the same prospects: the same honour's and the same rewards; and without hypocrisy this constitution of the United States of America, meant just what it said, without reference to color or condition . . . equal rights, as appears in said constitution, ought to be treated by those to whom the administration of the laws are entrusted . . .
>
> Petition also, ye goodly inhabitants of the slave states, your legislators to abolish slavery by the year 1850, or now, and save the abolitionist from reproach and ruin, infamy and shame. Pray Congress to pay every man a reasonable price for his slaves out of the surplus revenue arising from the sale of public lands and from the deduction of pay from the members of Congress. Break off the shackles from the poor black man and hire him to labor like other human beings: for "an hour of virtuous liberty on earth is worth a whole eternity of bondage."[39]
>
> —Joseph Smith

---

39. Joseph Smith, "Truth Will Prevail," in *Times and Seasons* [Nauvoo, IL], May 15, 1844, vol. V, no. 10.

Chapter XI: It Will All Be Worth It

The precipitating event of Joseph's murder came about a month after his views on slavery were published in the Times and Seasons newspaper.

Jane reports, "I shall never forget that time of agony and sorrow. When he was killed, I liked to a died myself . . . I was sick abed, and the teachers told me. 'You don't want to die because he did, He died for us, and now we all want to live and do all the good we can.'"[40]

Jane acutely felt the tragedy of what had happened. She had been residing with Joseph, his wife, Emma Smith, and his mother, Lucy Mac Smith, in the Nauvoo Mansion House around the time of his death. She knew Joseph Smith well and reported that even before meeting him, she had a dream detailing his physical features.[41] At the time, Emma Smith had invited Jane to be adopted as a daughter into the Smith family through a temple ordinance for the eternities. Jane declined the offer and, after Joseph Smith's death, lived in Brigham Young's household, who succeeded him as leader of the Church. Later in life, dictating a letter with the aid of fellow pioneer Elizabeth Roundy, Jane wrote to Church leader John Taylor, explaining that she was "so green"[42] to have not understood the significance of what the ordinance implied, and requested that Emma Smith's temple offer be honored. That request was ultimately denied. Ensuing twenty years, Jane wrote letters to Church presidents for temple access and ordinances that were not granted in her lifetime.

After Joseph Smith's antislavery address and assassination, Church leaders became more vocal, simultaneously distancing themselves from and refusing to establish policies regarding black membership and participation in the Church. Statements in the early nineteenth century in a divided world of blacks and whites in social and religious traditions were very apparent in both secular and church writings. Some reiterated widespread discriminatory beliefs of the day,

---

40. Susa Young Gates, "Aunt Jane James," *Young Women Journal*, vol. XVI, 553.
41. Arnold K. Garr, Donald Q. Cannon, Richard O, Cowan, and John M. Bernheisel, *Encyclopedia of Latter-day Saint History* (Salt Lake City, UT: Deseret Book, 2000), 97.
42. Henry J. Wolfinger, *A Test of Faith: Jane Elizabeth James and the Origins of the Utah Black Community*, Special Collections, Harold B. Lee Library, Brigham Young University, Provo, UT.

including ideas of a divine curse on blacks, used to support the legally profitable enterprise of free labor in the transatlantic slave trade.

In his living days, even Joseph Smith had expressed these ideas when a mob manifesto, fearing slave uprisings, persecuted the Church for sentiments of racial integration.

The Church's printing press was destroyed, homes were burned, and members of The Church of Jesus Christ of Latter-Day Saints – were chased out of Missouri. Debates which separated the races, whether in worldly or religious circles, often centered on ideas of civility and savagery, privileges and rites, blessings and curses, particularly when discussing whether a person was biologically, socially, or divinely assigned to a specific race and order. In my thesis research, I couldn't find Church materials that explicitly denounced discriminatory comments from past Church prophets and apostles or supported what I felt was spiritually true. I believed blessings and potential curses resulted from how close or far away a person strove with God and was not based on race or skin color. I lived in Utah for several years and had grown to love its people. However, I became affected by stressful experiences of racial bias in the workplace, my studies, and my religion, and I felt left to my own devices to wrestle my circumstances alone.

It will all be worth it.

To use Jane's words, I, too, became "sick abed." It didn't help that during my years at
BYU, I had a severe case of chronic fatigue. Despite my weakened condition, on January 21st
2005, I felt a persistent, spiritual instruction to get out of bed and go to the LDS Film Festival held within walking distance at the Provo City Library. I eventually did, but not without complaining. Stuck in a cycle of reduced health and negative experiences, I told Heavenly Father that I was fed up with Utah and didn't have any energy to reach out to people. Shaking with weakness as I dressed, I told Him that if He wanted me to talk to anyone, He would need to have that person sit right beside me. Since I didn't know why the Lord wanted me to be there, I brought a draft of my documentary thesis on black pioneers and my résumé in case either became relevant.

The meeting was like something out of a black-and-white detective movie. Moodily, I sat in front of a large movie screen, and sure enough, a person sat beside me and began talking with no introduction like we were finishing off an earlier conversation. She said, "They're not sure whether to include Jane." Jane kept being put in and removed from the film script. When I asked why that was the case, she replied that Jane's story was thought to be too trivial. While keeping my eyes on the movie neither of us seemed to be watching (in true secret-agent fashion), I said, "They need to. People need to know there were black pioneers."

At intermission, I recognized the lady I had been talking to as being involved in Church films. I showed her my manuscript, and she gave me the name of a documentary filmmaker who might be interested. I also left her with my acting résumé and went home. Two months later, on March 8th, I was at the BYU Student Health Center for two scheduled doctor's appointments. I was early, which wasn't like me, and I had time to look at emails on one of the computers at the health center. I saw two emails from the audio and visual casting producer for a Joseph Smith movie the Church was making – the same lady I had met at the film festival. One had been sent to me individually, and the other as part of a mailing list). The emails were invitations to audition for the role of Jane Manning James, which, to my surprise, was taking place that day in a few hours. I immediately canceled my doctor's appointments, walked to BYU to download the script, and took a bus to the LDS Motion Picture Studio, using the journey as an opportunity to practice my lines and American accent with two strangers, one white and the other black, whom I'd met separately along the way. The audition turned out to be the best I'd ever given, and I was elated to be given the role. My work visa, like my student visa, came at the eleventh hour, just before I was flown out to Canada to be filmed for Jane's scene.

When the movie production wrapped up, the casting producer sent me an email in which she noted that Heavenly Father must have known long ago that Jane was to be in the film. She felt I was led and inspired to attend the LDS Film Festival to serve as a direct reminder of Jane. She thanked me for being prepared and commented on the fact that I even had my résumé. She felt I was the perfect individual to play a valuable role. Little did she know how hard it had been for me to be in the right place at the right time or how hard it was to respond to her.

It took me seven years to respond to her email. My physical health deteriorated considerably. This pioneer had fallen off the back of the wagon, and, like Jane, I had to dictate my email to a missionary, who acted as my scribe. By 2015, after sending my email in 2013, an article titled "Race and the Priesthood" on the Church's website declared: "Today, the Church disavows the theories advanced in the past that black skin is a sign of divine disfavor or curse, or that it reflects unrighteous actions in a premortal life; that mixed-race marriages are a sin; or that blacks or people of any other race or ethnicity are inferior in any way to anyone else. Church leaders today unequivocally condemn all racism, past and present, in any form."[43]

Not once had I felt cursed. I felt blessed in my skin. However, not everyone felt that way. Many faithful members left the Church while others will not join due to its racial history, which, as with other churches and religions, will always be in print. Troubling racist statements from the past oftentimes relentlessly affect our future. Though this detailed inclusive race relations statement from the Church was not made from the pulpit, as some statements on race in the past were made, it was a Church statement I welcomed as I had sought it in my BYU studies a decade previous. What of now?

Reverend Lawrence Edward Carter Senior., founding dean of the Martin Luther King Jr. International Chapel, traveled to Salt Lake City and announced: 'Be it known to all who look upon this script that President Russell Marion Nelson Sr., MD, PhD, the 17th president of the Church of Jesus Christ of Latter-day Saints is being honoured" and he presented Nelson with a Peace Award. Carter praised Nelson's "Radical inclusivity."[44] A quote from his pre-recorded presentation

---

43. Gospel Topics Essays, "Race and the Priesthood," Gospel Library.

44. Sydney Walker, "Morehouse College honors President Nelson with peace prize, announces collaboration with Tabernacle Choir," *Church News*, Apr. 13, 2023, https://www.thechurchnews.com/leaders/2023/4/13/23682815/president-nelson-gandhi-king-mandela-peace-prize-morehouse-college-atlanta-tabernacle-choir/.

shown during an interfaith event in Atlanta on April 13th, 2023, reads as follows:

"We are honored to announce you as the inaugural laureate of the Morehouse College Gandhi-King-Mandela Peace Prize as an internationally recognized medical scientist, revered President, Prophet, Seer, and Revelator for the 17,000,000-member church of Jesus Christ of the Latter-day Saints. You have continued the legacy of Joseph Smith, founder of the Latter-day Saints movement and the first nationally recognized religious leader in the United States to advocate for the freedom of enslaved Africans by affirming racial and ethnic equality and running for the American presidency on a political platform of compensation emancipation."

President Nelson, speaking on many public platforms, encouraged members of the Church to "be one" ("Doctrine and Covenants 38:27") and 'lead out in abandoning attitudes and actions of prejudice.'[45] When seeking scripture on racial or gender equality, 2nd Nephi 26:33 from The Book of Mormon is often shared: ". . . he [the Lord] doeth nothing save it be plain unto the children of men; and he inviteth them all to come unto him and partake of his goodness; and he denieth none that come unto him, black and white, bond and free, male and female . . ."

The words "black," "white," "bond," and "free" were translated by Joseph Smith in the Book of Mormon and then later used in his presidential platform address on the emancipation of slaves. However, other "plain" verses in the book referencing "black" or "white" "skin," are often hastily skipped over, or encouraged to be read symbolically only, as they appear to be linked to worthiness before God through "colorism," an ideology used back when "racism" was thought by some to be a modern construct. A more complete treatise of this is outside of the scope of this article, but suffice it to say that it's important for me to wrestle on such topics as I feel my church membership is worth it.

---

45. Sarah Jane Weaver, "President Nelson calls upon Latter-day Saints 'to lead out in abandoning attitudes and actions of prejudice,'" *Church News*, Oct. 4, 2020, https://www.thechurchnews.com/2020/10/4/23217103/general-conference-october-2020-sunday-morning-session-president-nelson-race-prejudice-equality/.

The phrase "It will all be worth it" has been repeated in this article through events shared in my life. "It" is so often overlooked as it leans into the formula of hope, the formula of overcoming. But "it" is a hard thing or a series of events and experiences that are difficult. "Worth it" isn't possible with understanding experientially the difficulties that the first "it" holds for us.

Despite that, "it will all be worth it" is a hopeful phrase that elicits an encouraging response to those difficult situations. You were invited to walk with me on a journey of how one pioneer of the 21st century finds another from the 20th century–past and present–structured in a narrative that could, in fact, be both my story and your story combined.

My background is diverse, as likely is yours. I am of the African diaspora, of Jamaican origins, born in England with Scottish and African ancestry dating as far back as the slave ships that headed to the West Indies on the Caribbean South American continent. In my transformation to Jane, I readily acknowledge that I, with some of the audience members, may have felt separated from Jane in that I come from a different century, country, and racial history. However, several spiritual experiences informed me I would be playing the role of Jane. I felt called, and that my journey to portraying Jane in theatre and film was an interpretive bridge to help modern audiences understand Jane on a more personal and meaningful level.

With crucial racial interpretations of modern and ancient history hanging in the balance, many wonder why I, with others, could be in a Church with a history of racial prejudice and restriction. The truth is, I have a testimony that if Christ himself could choose to work with Apostles in his lifetime who were so imperfect, who am I not to reconsider such human frailties along the way? We are not at the very end or in a one-act play.

The reality is that the title of this article gave me the strength to write the article itself.

The hope, expectation, and confidence hold that, ultimately, through sacrifice and persistence, "it"–that challenge, that hard thing– will lead to something worth the sacrifice. In faith, I felt that God was with me throughout. Indeed, I can say that often, in my hardest trials,

I sensed a thinning of the veil, a change in the room, and a spiritual realm within reach.

Everything will be okay in the end. If it's not okay, it's not the end.

I was denied entry on the plane to Utah, but Jane was denied passage on a boat to Nauvoo. An officer demanded that Jane show "free papers" she didn't possess or need, and I knew that I had been told by an officer to go home to "get my papers in order." I may not have returned to Utah to be "free," but I did arrive to portray her, to represent her. The seven years I lived, studied, and worked in Utah were truly one of the most productive and fulfilling seasons of my life. Portraying Jane in theatre and film was an opportunity to bring her out of obscurity as a voice from the past and present her to modern audiences as she was known in life, as prominent member of the Church having lived with Joseph Smith and Brigham Young.

Driven by religious conviction, Jane truly was an individual who believed she belonged, and no one seemed to divest her of that belief. In her final recorded testimony, she concludes: "I want to say right here, that my faith in the Gospel of Jesus Christ as taught by the Church of Jesus Christ of Latter-day Saints is as strong today, nay, it is if possible stronger than it was the day I was first baptized. I pay my tithes and offerings, keep the Word of Wisdom, I go to bed early and rise early, I try in my feeble way to set a good example to all."[46]

Jane demonstrated spiritual intelligence by referring to the Church as a vehicle for the gospel of Christ. I believe she understood that in the Church, the gospel is taught through imperfect individuals in an imperfect world and that aspects of the true gospel of Christ are revealed incrementally – and occasionally restrained – precept by precept according to the conditions or dictates of the telestial realm in which we live. James Baldwin, a Black American writer and civil rights activist, said, "The great force of history comes from the fact

---

46. James Goldberg, "The Autobiography of Jane Manning James: Seven Decades of Faith and Devotion," *Church History*, accessed Mar. 16, 2024, https://history.churchofjesuschrist.org/content/pioneers-in-every-land/the-autobiography-of-jane-manning-james.

that we carry it within us."⁴⁷ As we consider Jane's story and the stories of other pioneers past and present as to whether their stories are of worth, or belong in mainstream history, perhaps one day there will be a demonstrable desire for a more complete truth in history, and it will be such that there will be no seats left in the house.

---

47. Peter Jennings and Todd Brewster, *In Search of America* (New York: Hyperion, 2002), 3.

XII
Divine Perspective

By Boyd Matheson

In all the trials, challenges, and experiences of life, we often don't know if such experiences are necessarily good or bad at the beginning. We just know they are hard. We know they are discouraging. We know that sometimes it hurts inside just to be awake. Sometimes even the good days can be consumed with questions about whether the effort and exertion to get on, stay on, or return to the covenant path is worth it.

The phrase "it will all be worth it" cannot be properly viewed through the lens that frames experience as awful, painful, frustrating, white-knuckle "holding on to the end" in the hope of some great reward. Rather, "it will all be worth it" is a way of living and a way of being and approaching every aspect of life, including questions, faith, trials, and success.

It *will* be worth it—and it *is* worth it—every day, every moment, when we begin to gain proper perspective, look to and hold on to Jesus Christ, and recognize that He has a place for us within His outstretched arms.

With that in mind, I wondered: Of so many possible readers, who should I write to? The wavering and struggling, the faithful and striving, the more senior souls, the youth, the women, the men, the married, the single, the successful, the weary, the wounded, the doubting, the faithful? The possibilities are endless. I have also wondered if there was a message for just the plain average follower of Jesus.

Years ago, as a newly called bishop, I was preparing for our ward conference and had questions about who, out the 424 members in our ward family, I should address my remarks to in our sacrament service.

As I was struggling to prepare, I felt impressed to send out a message to everyone in the Ward asking them to text or email me their name to me in ALL CAPS (and for parents to include the names of younger children). I didn't explain why, and honestly, I didn't really know myself. I just asked the members to trust me, and the resulting experience changed me forever.

As I saw each name appear on my phone in the days leading up to the conference, I smiled, remembering the many great memories I shared with these amazing neighbors and friends. I felt gratitude and thankfulness for their service, their lessons, and their testimonies. I reflected on their discipleship, each one, as they appeared on my phone and I was filled with a sense of humility, admiration, and excitement. The week was filled with deep spiritual impressions never to be forgotten.

As wonderful as that was, it was not the purpose of the exercise.

I came to the realization that I needed to pray not for *all* of the members of the ward but for *each* of them. Coming to understand the difference between *all* and *each* was soul-stirring and transformational.

Throughout the day, as each name would pop up in capital letters, I would say the name out loud for the Lord to hear, in a simple, sincere prayer. For those who may not have seen my message in their inbox or weren't able to respond, I went through and said their name out loud for the Lord to hear, in the same simple, sincere prayer. All were included, each individually acknowledged before God. And the Lord answered in every single instance.

Later, I recalled a radio interview I once conducted with Todd Rose about his book *The End of Average*. Rose used as his premise an example from the US Air Force in the 1950s. Crashes and poor pilot performance were devastating the organization. After blaming pilots, instructors, commanders, and a team of researchers began to look at the design of the cockpits.

Cockpits were being created to fit the average size of a typical Air Force pilot based on ten physical dimensions. Over 4,000 airmen had their measurements taken and logged.

To the surprise of most on the research team, out of the over 4,000 pilots measured, not a single one fit the average on all ten dimensions. Some pilots had long torsos but shorter arms; others had bigger shoulders but shorter legs. The big discovery was that there really was no such thing as an average pilot. In designing a cockpit to fit the average pilot, they were actually designing a cockpit to fit no one at all.

Rose concluded that mass-producing doesn't really work. Because there is no average—ever!

Likewise, our joy and salvation cannot be mass-produced. When it comes to sons and daughters of heavenly parents, there is no average—ever. There is only distinctness and divine potential. There *is* no average follower of Jesus Christ. We are each unique an unlike anyone else. Christ knows each of us individually. We say that so often it can feel impersonal or cliche, but He suffered for you. If you were the only one who chose to be saved, He still would have suffered everything just to save you, imperfect, struggling you, because He knows what your future has in store for you. He has prepared it, just for you. Three scripture stories help us see the individual connection He hopes to have with each of us.

On the first Easter morning, Mary wept and mourned inconsolably before the empty tomb. So great was her grief that even when Jesus asked, "Why weepest thou?" Mary thought him to be the gardener. It wasn't until the Savior called Mary by name that her fears, sadness, and sorrows were swept away and she beheld the resurrected Jesus.

When the Savior appeared to the Nephites, He invited them to come forth one by one to see and feel the prints of the nails in His hands and feet. One by one they came. In visualizing that scene of scenes, it is my belief that the Savior greeted each of them by name as they came to see, sense, and know for themselves that He was and is their personal Redeemer.

Likewise, it is no small thing that when the young Joseph Smith prayed in a grove we call sacred, his record of that heavenly vision states, "I saw two Personages, whose brightness and glory defy all description, standing above me in the air. One of them spake unto me, *calling me by name* and said, pointing to the other—This is My Beloved Son. Hear Him!" (Joseph Smith—History 1:17; emphasis added).

That moment changed the world forever. In that vision, the young prophet learned that Heavenly Father knew him by name and that God desired to have him hear Jesus.

It isn't necessary for us to have a vision in order to gain such knowledge about our relationship with Christ. But we do have to have experiences with the Divine to help us understand who we are and whose we are. Gaining that knowledge gives us confidence to face life and brings joy and happiness to our daily routine.

As we come to know both who we are and whose we are, we will experience more confidence, more holiness, more joy, more love, more personal peace—in short, just more. That will be worth it!

That's not to say that coming to this understanding frees us from doing all the things we know will help us progress on the covenant path. The Buddha is purported to have taught an important principle, saying, "Before enlightenment—chop wood, carry water. After enlightenment—chop wood, carry water." In other words, even when we come to truly understand our divine worth and identity, ministering still matters, lessons still need preparing, the holy Sabbath still needs keeping, scriptures still need to be read, and prayers still need to be said—not because Heavenly Father needs us to validate His self-esteem but because we need moments to remember, and be reminded through the Spirit, who we truly are.

President Russell M. Nelson knows who and whose we are. The prophet recently admonished, "Brothers and sisters, as covenant children of God, give Him a fair share of your time, every day. As you do, you will learn about His power to comfort, strengthen, renew, and heal you."⁴⁸ That is a promise worth proving.

He has called to you today, saying, "Fear not: for I have redeemed thee, I have called thee by thy name; thou art mine" (Isaiah 43:1).

A Perspective on Perspective

Growing up, I was obsessed with basketball and was certain I would fulfill my dream of playing in college. I practiced more hours than I could count, and as a senior in high school I felt my dream could actually come true.

Everything was going just perfect . . . until it wasn't. As my senior season progressed, my right shoulder began to fall apart. It got to the point where it would dislocate whenever it wanted to. (If you have ever had the experience of waking up in the morning on one side of your bed and find your shoulder over on the other, you know the pain and challenge it brings.)

After being examined by the doctor, I was informed that I needed to have surgery. I was also bluntly told that the chances of me ever playing competitive basketball again would be slim to none. This wasn't fair! I remember feeling like the one thing that had become such a big part of my identity was being ripped away. It plunged me into deep discouragement. I felt so alone. It seemed like no one understood what I was going through.

One night, a neighbor, Elder Hugh Pinnock—then a member of The Quorum of the Seventy—called and asked if I could come over to his house. I had no idea why he would want to talk to me, but I agreed and drove over. He met me at the door with no smile, no welcome, not even a handshake. He led me back to his den, we sat down, and he told me this story:

> A long time ago, there was an old man who lived in a very small village. The only possession he had was a strong and beautiful horse. The

---

48. Sarah Jane Weaver, "During special broadcast, President Nelson asks California members to seek truth, make and keep covenants, gather Israel," *Church News*, Feb. 27, 2022, https://www.thechurchnews.com/2022/2/27/23216727/president-nelson-california-devotional-invitations-seek-truth-make-and-keep-covenants-gather-israel.

horse was his only means for providing for himself and his family. One night, a great storm arose with thunder and lightning. The horse was frightened and ran feverishly about the corral. As the storm continued, the gate to the corral was blown open and the horse bolted and ran off into the desert.

The next morning, the people of the village gathered together to take inventory of the damage from the storm. Upon hearing that the old man had lost his horse, the people of the village went to his humble home. All the people went up to the man, saying, "This is a sad day. You have lost your only possession and the only means that you had to take care of your family. This is awful and truly terrible." The old man looked at the people and softly replied, "You do not know that this is bad; you do not know that this is terrible."

The days went by, and one night the horse returned and brought with it fifty wild horses it had been running with out in the desert. The people of the village again gathered themselves at the cottage of the old man. The people exclaimed, "This is so wonderful and good. Now that you have all of these horses and all this wealth, you will never have another worry. What a great and wonderful thing!" The old man faced the crowd and whispered, "You do not know that this is a wonderful thing; you do not know that this is good."

The old man had a son who was one of the great young warriors in the village. He spent hours training to perfect his skills with the sword and the slingshot. One day as he was breaking in one of the new horses, he was thrown from the horse and his leg was crushed. Never again would he be able to use the skills he had worked so hard to acquire. When the people of the village heard the news, they responded again by saying, "This great young warrior is crippled; what an awful, terrible thing." The old man responded, "You do not know that this is terrible; you do not know that this is a bad thing."

Not long after the tragic incident, the cry of war was heard in the land, and the warlords came to the village and took all the able young men off to battle, and the majority of them were killed.

That was the end of the story. Elder Pinnock challenged me to remember the story, stood up, and escorted me out of the house. I remember driving home wondering what in the world this was all about. I was waiting for Paul Harvey to come on the radio with his famous song "The Rest of the Story," but that *was* the story.

After I had my surgery, I remember sitting in the hospital room, and as my friends, family, and coaches came to visit, they all would say, "Oh, Boyd, this is so bad. Here you have spent all these years practicing and training and now it's over. What an awful, terrible thing."

Without even thinking, I replied, "No, you don't know this is bad; you don't know this is a terrible thing!"

Truly it wasn't! In fact, it was one of the best things that ever happened to me. During the long hours and days of recovery and physical therapy, I had a shift in focus. It created the opportunity for me to set some goals and focus on things that were far more important than making baskets or winning championships. It forever changed who I was and who I would strive to become.

Everything was perfect until it wasn't—and then it got better and was absolutely worth it!

Perspective is a choice. Sometimes we need to change our perspective about perspective. Maintaining proper perspective is a skill that can be developed.

It's important to remember that in the face of daunting, difficult challenges, we may not know if they are good or bad, though we certainly know they are tough and can seem overwhelming. Framing our perspective properly can be a first step to moving forward. There might just be an opportunity in the midst of that ominous experience.

For those who may find themselves at the bottom of a black hole of depression, discouragement, or despair, remember that it is against the laws of nature—and nature's God—that storms last forever. Storms come and then go, and with the right perspective they can be a good thing—a renewing, cleansing, and empowering experience. Hard? Yes! Painful? Yes! Frightening? Yes! Worth enduring? Yes! There is hope in perspective.

*

If you are ever struggling to know or remember your worth, if at any time on any day you are in need of a prayer, *please* send me an email with your name, in all caps![49]

---

49. My email address is boyd@trilliumstrategies.com. And yes, that *is* my personal email!

Hanging On by a Thread

One of the most powerful scenes from the political classic *The West Wing*. It occurred in an episode when the president's chief of staff, Leo McGarry (a recovering alcoholic), reached out to a struggling staffer, Josh Lyman. McGarry waited for Lyman while he attended a counseling session.

When Lyman finished his counseling session, he asked the often surly McGarry why he had waited hours for him to come out. McGarry responded with a story:

> This guy is walking down a street when he falls in a hole. The walls are so steep that he can't get out. A doctor passes by and the guy shouts up, "Hey you! Can you help me out?" The doctor writes a prescription, throws it down in the hole, and moves on. Then a priest comes along and the guy shouts up, "Father, I'm down in this hole! Can you help me out?" The priest writes out a prayer, throws it down in the hole, and moves on. Finally, a friend walks by. "Hey Joe, it's me! Can you help me out?" And the friend jumps in the hole. Our guy says, "Are you stupid? Now we're both down here." The friend says, "Yeah, but I've been down here before . . . and I know the way out!"[50]

You are not alone—there are many of us who have been in the bottom of that big black hole. We know the way out. Hanging on and holding on leads to hope and healing—and that is always worth it.

I was texting with a dear friend who, through no fault of her own, was in the middle of a gut-wrenching, soul-searing series of infuriatingly unfair trials. She is one of the strongest and most faithful souls I know. She confided that while she was keeping her faith, at times she felt like was hanging on by a thread.

Without thinking, I was impressed to reply, "A thread is all the Savior needs. And as long as we hold on to our end of that thread, He will forever hold on to His end, and that thread will bind us to Him like a mighty cord."

---

50. Thomas Schlamme, "Noël," *The West Wing*, season 2, episode 10, NBC, 2000, https://www.imdb.com/title/tt0745664/characters/nm0817983.

One Sunday morning I was in the bishop's office praying, and again this same thought came to my mind about my friend who felt she was hanging by a thread. I looked up at a New Testament painting I had on the wall depicting the woman who had suffered twelve grueling years with a blood condition that had clearly exhausted her physically, monetarily, spiritually, and emotionally. It could be said that the faith and future of that certain New Testament woman were indeed hanging by a thread.

Matthew 9:20–22 reads:

> And, behold, a woman, which was diseased with an issue of blood twelve years, came behind him, and touched the hem of his garment:
>
> For she said within herself, If I may but touch his garment, I shall be whole.
>
> But Jesus turned him about, and when he saw her, he said, Daughter, be of good comfort; thy faith hath made thee whole. And the woman was made whole from that hour.

I love how in this particular painting, the woman who had been sick and suffering is holding on to a thread from the hem of the Savior's garment. In the pressing crowd that followed Jesus to see if he would heal Jairus's dying daughter, the woman had simply grasped a thread. Fortunately for her, all the Savior needed was for her to catch hold of a thread. The weaving together of her faith and His compassionate power would heal and bless her, and her act has inspired faith and hope in so many others for over two thousand years.

Like a strand of golden thread, Elder Holland wrote, "To any who may be struggling to see that light and find that hope, I say: Hold on. Keep trying. God loves you. Things will improve."[51] Such a golden thread is hope-filled and spirit-spun and will bind the humble holder of the other end to Jesus. Elder Holland is truly a weaver of threads for all to hold on to in difficult days or trying times.

Likewise, President Nelson declared to those hanging on by a thread, "Dear friends, the road ahead may be bumpy, but our

---

51. Jeffrey R. Holland, "An High Priest of Good Things to Come," *Ensign*, Nov. 1999, 36.

destination is serene and secure. So, fasten your seatbelt, hang on through the bumps, and do what's right. Your reward will be eternal."[52]

Prophets and apostles, leaders and friends, ministers and neighbors can provide such strengthening threads for us to grasp as can temple worship, scriptures, and humble prayer. The veil often parts with heavenly threads fluttering in the spiritual breeze for us to reach for and grab on to.

When you find yourself feeling as though you are hanging on by a thread, *hold on*! A thread is all the Savior needs, and as long as you hold on to your end, He will forever hold on to His.

THE SAVIOR'S OUTSTRETCHED ARMS

I was powerfully reminded recently, by an extraordinarily resilient departing missionary, of the significance of the Lord's arms being ever extended wide after us. The Savior's merciful arms are outstretched even (and especially) when we may feel lost, forsaken, or left alone.

I have reflected on the belief that the sacred space between the Savior's arms is exactly the size and shape of our broken hearts, battered lives, wounded souls, and weary minds. Jesus ever widens the welcome to encircle us in His eternal, loving embrace.

Elder Neil L. Andersen once taught that "The scriptures speak of His arms being open, extended, stretched out, and encircling. They are described as mighty and holy, arms of mercy, arms of safety, arms of love, 'lengthened out all the day long.'"[53]

In his 2022 general conference address, Elder Jeffrey R. Holland poignantly proclaimed, "It is one of the most powerful paradoxes of the Crucifixion that the arms of the Savior were stretched wide open and then nailed there, unwittingly but accurately portraying that every man, woman, and child in the entire human family is not only welcome but invited into His redeeming, exalting embrace."[54]

As part of a media team following President Nelson's Global Ministry Tour, I caught a glimpse of what "it will all be worth it"

---

52. Russell M. Nelson, "As we are now many months," Facebook, Aug. 5, 2020, https://www.facebook.com/russell.m.nelson/posts/3188508891216525.

53. Neil L. Andersen, "Repent . . . That I May Heal You," *Ensign*, Nov. 2009, 40.

54. Jeffrey R. Holland, "Lifted Up upon the Cross," *Liahona*, Nov. 2022, 79.

looks like. After a devotional with a large gathering in South America, President Nelson came down from the stand to shake hands with special guests and dignitaries. As he worked his way down the line of visitors, the world seemed to stand still when a little boy couldn't be held back and ran toward President Nelson. The jailbreak was on, and a number of other Primary children enthusiastically followed.

Before anyone else knew what to do, the prophet dropped to his knees and scooped the children up into his outstretched arms. On his knees, the prophet held the future of a nation in his arms. He widened the welcome and encircled the little ones as he gathered them into his loving embrace.

Elder Andersen tenderly described his interaction with President Thomas S. Monson after receiving his call to the apostleship, saying, "I will forever remember his kindness as he extended my call last April. At the conclusion of our interview, he opened his arms to embrace me. President Monson is a tall man. As he wrapped his long arms around me and pulled me close, I felt like a little boy being held in the protective arms of a loving father." Reflecting on such a singular moment, Elder Andersen continued, "In the months since that experience, I have thought of the Lord's invitation to come unto Him and to spiritually be wrapped in His arms. He said, 'Behold, [my arms] of mercy [are] extended towards you, and whosoever will come, him will I receive; and blessed are those who come unto me.'"[55]

As if managing a house with eleven children wasn't raucous, challenging, and crazy enough, my parents were forever widening the welcome to anyone who needed a place to eat, a place to stay, or a place to sleep. I realized years later that the large number of individuals drawn into our home weren't really there for the wonderful food or safe shelter—they were there because of the wide welcome and loving arms my parents extended as they emulated the Savior, Jesus Christ. The space between my parents' arms and the space within the Savior's reach provided each soul a moment to recognize there was a place for them.

Alma taught, "Thus the Lord did begin to pour out his Spirit upon them; and we see that his arm is extended to all people" (Alma 19:36). "Behold, he sendeth an invitation unto all men, for the arms of mercy

---

55. Neil L. Andersen, "Repent . . . That I May Heal You," 40.

are extended towards them" (Alma 5:33). And Nephi exclaimed, "I am encircled about eternally in the arms of his love" (2 Nephi 1:15).

Our hearts, homes, chapels, and conversations should all be places to widen the welcome and create sacred space in between. President Jeffrey R. Holland eloquently stated, "May I be bold enough to suggest that it is impossible for anyone who really knows God to doubt his willingness to receive us with open arms in a divine embrace if we will but 'come unto Him.'"[56]

Jesus Christ stands at the gates of our days, our lives, and eternity with open arms, declaring, "I will encircle thee in the arms of my love" (Doctrine and Covenants 6:2). Even if stumbling or staggering, we can fall into his outstretched arms, feel His love, and know that the space between His arms has been consecrated, through His loving atoning sacrifice, as a place for us. That will be worth it all.

Knowing who we are, gaining proper perspective, looking to and holding on to Jesus, and finding our place within His outstretched arms is worth it! Every single day—on every path, through every place, in every space we find ourselves during our mortal sojourn—it is all worth it!

---

56. Jeffrey R. Holland, "Come unto Me" (Brigham Young University devotional, Mar. 2, 1997), 3, speeches.byu.edu.

XIII

From Bad, to Worse, to Even Worse

By Al Carraway

I've always felt a closeness with Old Testament Joseph. Visions of being a leader with parents who favored him—life was good. You know, until it wasn't. Abandoned in a hole, sold as a slave by his own brothers, to spending years in prison. His life seemed to go from bad, to worse, to even worse. It was as if all of those blessings he had been promised were wishful thinking.

Personally, when I was growing up, life was so good. But as it turns out, following my baptism in my twenties, the good times were painfully, clearly over. Right now, 15 years later, I continue to feel like I'm in Joseph's outline of bad, to worse, to even worse.

After my baptism, I experienced a deep, deep reconstruction and rewiring of myself as I worked to abandon 21 years of habits, traditions, and culture that made up my entire existence. As if that wasn't painfully hard already, I found myself at a crossroad, needing to choose between my faith and all of my friends and family. It was them or God. But how does someone make that kind of choice? Was the God I just met worth giving up those who had always been there for me? Who had raised me and loved me? Those I loved?

It was a really hard decision, but I chose God. I spent years without hearing anything from my family, literal years of silence with no reunion from any of those friends. When I thought God could not require any more from me, He prompted me to move across the country to a place I'd never been, where I didn't know a single person. But I went. I left behind the only way of living that I knew of, coping with the possibility that I may never see my family again, and immediately after arriving, things went from bad to worse.

I had never known loneliness like I did moving across the country. The sense of sacrifice and loss made me feel an indescribable anguish where my body would physically ache. The judgment I felt was immobilizing, and so many times, I yelled in prayer until I lost my voice. There were times I thought my faith and my God were failing me because of the unwanted, unexpected, and uncharted life choices that I felt He was consistently calling me to go down.

Make no mistake, I'm not trying to say that my conversion caused any of this, but if I am to trace back to the start of disruption, it would make its way to the font.

So then, what of Joseph? How did his series of unwanted turns and even worse life events pan out? Did his life continue in the pattern of unwanted events getting worse and worse? Did his life continue in what seemed like a series of missed blessings, broken promises, and ignored desires?

He did in fact become a leader, just as he always felt he would be. But, instead of being a leader of his small area over his own family, he was a leader over all of Egypt! He literally saved an entire civilization. And not only was he reunited with his family, but he was able to bring all of them to something better, a better way of living in every aspect. The hole, the slavery, the prison, the passing time, all of it had led him to these greater things that were intricately part of it all to begin with. Not only was it all fulfilled, but magnified! The promises were greater than Joseph had ever dreamed of, despite the fact that he had been shown them in a dream.

God was not overlooking or ignoring or punishing. In fact, He was working hard with every little detail to be sure it was even better

Chapter XIII: From Bad, to Worse, to Even Worse

than what Joseph had in mind. All of it was part of the plan to begin with. It was all needed, necessary, and perfectly crafted by God for Joseph at every stage, in every season, and even in worst moments.

Following God's prompt in 2020, my husband, our kids, and I moved out of Arizona and tried buy a home back in New York. However, through a long series of events that went from bad to worse, we ultimately ended up not getting our house when we arrived across the country for the second time. Despite our consistent best efforts, we spent nearly two months without a home. My youngest at the time was less than a year old and learned to walk in a tiny hotel room that the five of us and a giant dog squeezed into, as our bank account was drained more and more with each night's stay.

Weeks passed as I was emotionally and spiritually depleted. I finally collapsed on the floor of the hotel room, my body aching from being stretched so thin. I told God from the floor, "I'm done. I got nothin' left." I had never felt so thin. My faith, my strength, my optimism were just done. I felt like I had been left out to dry. His response still stopped me in my tracks and leaves me marveling today:

"Why won't you let me bless you? Why won't you let me take you somewhere better? That's why I exist!"

He said that to me when we didn't have a home to live in. And He said that to me years previous when I didn't have my family. He said that to me during years of unemployment. He said that to me during a high-risk pregnancy when the odds were painfully against me. And He said that to me every time I wondered where He was and every time I collapsed on the ground with my pleadings and a weight I could no longer carry. Why won't you let me bless you?

It occurred to me that I was limiting a limitless God. I had placed restrictions on Him. I didn't mean to. But it occurred to me that my previous experience with God wasn't the only way to experience his love. I was holding on to what I knew so tightly that my knowledge was hindering me from learning what else I could experience. I had subconsciously put this box around Him and His spirit, telling myself how and when His Spirit and His answers could come to me. "I know how to get answers to my prayers, and they come in this box I created because every answer He had given me so far had come this way." And when it didn't come those ways, I felt like He wasn't there at all, or He didn't care. I was keeping myself from experiencing and recognizing His vastness.

I thought, who is God to me if I am not getting what I want? I shifted my gaze focus, and thoughts. What if He was answering me outside of that box that I ignorantly put there to begin with? When I tried to take away these limits that I subconsciously put on Deity, I began to notice and discover different ways God was answering my prayers and trying to guide me. His responses had just gone over my head. What seemed like unanswered prayers and rejection turned out to be Him rerouting me to better things than I had in mind. The times I thought God wasn't there, I found him in my blind spots. What appeared as God's distance was His intimate participation in my personal life. Everything I had been fighting against blossomed into my favorite things.

When I was writing my New Testament book, you know what part bothered me? Palm Sunday. Streets were lined with people, everyone was cheering Hosanna, and Jesus was welcomed like the king that He is. Only for just a few days later, those same people lined those same streets and watched Him walk to His death. I was so bothered wondering what happened?! What happened in such a short time that caused them to turn away from Him?! I wanted to be mad at them. But I couldn't. I'm them. I do this. I realized everyone was saying Hosanna for different reasons—some as believers, some thinking He would be the answer to political oppression, and others placing their hope in Him for military change over Roman enemies. They all had their own vision of what Jesus was going to do for them specifically. And then when it wasn't in their own limited ways, they turned away. And maybe I don't turn away completely like they did, but maybe just enough, that I turned to my own problem solving, my own path, my own ways.

My pregnancy was diagnosed as complicated and high-risk with an incredibly low survival rate when I was pregnant with my third. I passed seven months of that pregnancy in fear, but after seven months my doctor told me that I was fine. When I looked at him confused, he said he had never seen that happen before, but that there were no signs of any current or previous complications. I was fine. I left that appointment saying out loud to myself: God is good!

But . . . I hated that I felt that way. What did that imply? Was God just not good the other seven months of my pregnancy? Is God only good when we get what we want? Is the definition of a miracle dependent upon a possessive or happy outcome?

If miracles are dependent upon positive or desired outcomes, what does that say about Jesus? His whole life He was mocked and spit on and falsely judged and finally murdered. Was it because angels weren't there? Was it because God wasn't mindful of Him? Was it because Christ wasn't deserving of that prevention? Was it because God is not always good?

The greatest thing I have learned that has strengthened my relationship in tangible ways is that:

God is good even when our situation is not.

God is good in missed opportunities and passed time. God is good because He keeps His promises. He is good because He is aware; He is awake; He is conscious. God is good because He does not turn His back, close His eyes, neglect, or abandon His children. He is actively a part of every detail of our spiritual development. He does not play favorites. God is good even when our situation is not because we are a part of something so much bigger than our narrow-mindedness, so much bigger than what's here in front of our faces.

Like we see with Joseph and everyone else in scripture, he is not abandoned or overlooked. God was intricately and profoundly involved in bringing Joseph to a beautiful magnification.

If Christ would have prevented Lazarus from dying, mass conversion would have never happened. If Old Testament Joseph never went into a hole, to slavery, to prison, he never would have saved an entire civilization and become a leader of all Egypt. Lehi and his family didn't have to suffer in the wilderness, but their alternative was to witness the destruction and death of those in Jerusalem. If Jesus hadn't suffered the cross, the whole earth would have been for nothing. If I had never gone through what I experienced, I wouldn't have anything I have now.

The unexpected is God intervening.

One of my favorite scriptures is Isaiah speaking about the abuse Jesus endures: "it pleased the Lord to bruise him" (Isaiah 53:10). Why? Because there was, in fact, something so much more to come. God is good even when our situation is not, because He knows something we don't, something greater.

What if we got it all backward? What if every step is the miracle?

When Jesus finds Peter and asks him to leave everything behind, that isn't easy. It isn't compatible with his life. Peter has to change. But Christ should disrupt our lives. He should disrupt our own plans. He can change us if we let him. We should allow Him to disrupt and change us; that's the best part! The unexpected, unwanted, and uncharted parts of our lives represent His participation in our lives!

When we are willing to be like Peter on his failed night of fishing and say, "I will" before dropping our nets on the other side of the boat at the Lord's command, magnifications happen. Both our literal and figurative ships are filled to near sinking by His magnification!

Christ shows Peter that He is able to provide fish, but He doesn't want fish. He doesn't need fish. Fish are nothing. He wants you. And He wants to give you so much more than what's right here within reach. He wants to give you all that is better, all that is lasting, all that is good. "This is the will of Him that sent me" (John 6:40).

Peter is also a good example of how the adversary is most successful. Satan skews our perspective and thoughts. Satan tells us that Jesus is sleeping during our storms because He does not care. Lucifer is quick to point out our failures and focus on our slip ups, our sinkings, our shortcomings. And we go over them in our heads, what we are lacking, what we did wrong, and what we could have done differently.

It's true, right? That's what we do with Peter on the water. And that's what we do to ourselves. The adversary shifts our focus off the good, off the progress, off of Jesus and tells us that the waves are too big, the thunder is too loud, or that Jesus is too far, that what we are trying to do is too impossible.

When we lose our focus and then start believing Satan's lies, we fail; we feel our efforts are not good enough, or that we are not good enough. Satan gets us to feel bad about our efforts so we will stop making them. "Look how you failed. Look at what you did wrong. God is disappointed. Don't bother."

But Peter is the only one who gets off the boat. He is the only one who tries, the only one who steps out, the only one who walks on water with Jesus. And it brings Peter closer to Jesus.

He Who even the winds obey could have stopped the storm at any time, but He doesn't. In fact, Peter never would have even been on the boat in the first place if Jesus hadn't told him to go out on the boat. So, what if, it's not even about walking on water. What if, it's just about going to Him, during it all?

The adversary will tell us that Jesus is scolding Peter when He says, 'O thou of little faith, wherefore didst thou doubt?" But that is not how God sees you or your efforts. Wherefore didst thou doubt is not in response to Peter's sinking, but in direct response to Peter's pleadings to be saved!

"Lord, save me."

"Wherefore didst thou doubt?" As if He were saying, "Of course, I will save you, rescue you. How could you doubt that? I am right here. I am out here with you. Did you really think I was going to let the storm hurt you?"

Your efforts, your small steps forward may only seem like slip ups and failures, but you are in fact moving forward. You are doing something seemingly impossible. Even the slip ups and the smallest of steps are getting you closer to Jesus. As Peter knows, safety does not come from reaching for the boat. It comes from reaching for Him.

I collapsed under fatigue and pain from trials. I struggled so long that my body physically ached. It hurt. It was sore because the burden I was asked to bear was too big, too heavy, too impossible, too unwanted. I felt loss so painful that it caused me to yell loudly at God, to wonder where He was, and to lose my voice. I felt empty. I felt hallow and hopeless.

But never did a single pore of mine bleed from it.

The drops of blood falling from Jesus's pores are not figurative; they are literal. He gives all that He has to give. He holds nothing back. He gives it all so we can receive it all.

No mortal man could have withstood even a sliver of the weight that Christ felt in that garden. I can't imagine how feeling the weight and the consequences of every single soul to ever exist and that ever will exist must have felt. I sit here overwhelmed and fatigued just with myself. That moment of infinite pain and sorrow consumed His entirety, yet more was required of Him throughout the entire night. After the garden, He is dragged to five different locations like some sort of sick roadshow. His clothes are torn. "He is guilty of death," people around Him shout as they spit on Him. They blindfold Him and hit Him.

Upon the cross of calvary, they crucify Him. On a hill, by the most crowded roads, at a time of Passover when everyone is visiting Jerusalem, Jesus is made a spectacle for mockery, a target for stones and abuse. He is stripped of His clothes; His arms are stretched, and great mallets forcefully drive nails into His sinless flesh. The spikes are hammered through nerves and tendons in both His hands and His feet to make any movement excruciating throughout the entire body. Jesus does it willingly; He allows it to be done to Him. He does it for all those who believe on Him. And He does it for all those who don't.

He could have saved Himself from the cross, but He doesn't.

In one word, in one single command, He could have put an end to it all. And yet, He doesn't open His mouth to do so. What could have caused Jesus to allow Himself to endure any an even all of that?

You. Saving you. Getting you back. Giving you everything. He is motivated and strengthened by what He believes you can become.

He doesn't die because of Judas. He dies for Judas. He doesn't die because of Pharisees or the other Jewish leaders. He dies for them, and for you. The very people who place Him on the cross are the same people He is saving. He endures that brutality to save my soul, too.

The fact that Jesus chose the cross means Jesus chose you. It was always about and for you. He never looses sight of that. He never looses sight of you.

Jesus dies knowing that I might not ever want Him. What love.

I can live for that kind of love.

There will be times we'll wonder why Jesus does not exercise His power in our behalf. In those moments, we can remember that He did not always exercise it on His own behalf. "Ye shall be sorrowful," He says. And we can add pained, lonely, misunderstood, struggling, persecuted. "But your sorrow shall be turned into joy" (John 16:20).

Repentance isn't condemning, but the most optimistic and freeing thing there is, the ability and privilege to change, to start again, to try again. Because of repentance, we can be different, things can be different. Repentance makes it so that we are not stuck. We are not stagnant. Because of repentance, all is not lost; this is not final; we are not done. It means we have a God of commas, not periods.

It is such a privilege to have God intervene. To know He loves you so intimately that He is willing to cut in, to adjust, to re-shift, to redirect, and to give us life more abundantly. There is nothing He cannot fix. Darkness may come, but the sun always rises.

I was stretched so thin, depleted, empty, sunken in, but in the most unexpected ways, He has come and breathed life and revival into my sunken spots.

When I deplete from the weight of life, He breaths hope back into me.

When I sink from confusion, He inflates my life with peace.

When I collapse from struggles in darkness, He raises me with the renewal, revival, and light.

When I am shrinking, He brings swelling.

When I am empty, He brings fullness and plenty.

Like the expanding and contracting of a beating heart, with every fall comes the rise.

In our lives, we may find times were everything feels like their in pieces, but those pieces have created space for transformations and transitions so that life can be the best that has ever been and could ever be. I may collapse . . . a lot, but when I finally have it in me to open my eyes, I notice that it has always been at His feet.

Before Jesus was crucified, He knew the price of our sins was His death. He also knew the source of those sins were you and I. But He couldn't bear eternity without you, so He chose the cross. Like the prodigal son, the best rings and robes are waiting. And He is waiting to rejoice with you. How proud He is to be yours.

We don't always know the what or the why, but we do always know the Who, a God who is always good. Because He descended below it all, everything that brings us down, weighs us down, holds us down, can be lifted up. He can lift us all higher! He can lift and lighten our load, elevate us to greater heights above the storm clouds into beautiful magnifications that are promised to us. We will find peace to our soul. Everlasting struggle just isn't in the cards for us.

Your struggles aren't to break you down; they are to break you through. Take a chance on your good, reoccurring thoughts. Allow God, to be God. Embrace the unexpected knowing Who is guiding you. Small steps are still steps. Slow steps are still steps. And every step is a miracle. You are in route to the even better. And you will stand all amazed.

It is worth the disruption from He who gave all to us so that we can receive all. The feeling and ability to soar is worth it. These moments that cause our spirits to jolt and dance within us are worth it. The chance, the power, and the strength to be lifted up and out is worth it. He is worth it. Endless life and eternal bliss is worth it. Allow His ways to disrupt your life; that's the best part!

When Jesus fell in the garden, He was thinking of you. When He was on the cross, He was thinking of you. The love of Jesus never fails; it didn't in the garden, or on the cross. His love hasn't failed today, it won't fail tomorrow, or ever.

Never-ending happiness and endless bliss is the reality you are moving toward. It's in your future. He has always had every intention of giving it you, and he still intends to. Because you are His. And He's never lost sight of that. He's never lost sight of you.

It has always been about saving YOU, getting you back, giving you everything. So go, in peace because "thou shalt see greater things" (John 1:50).

XIV
BE STILL, TOGETHER
By Michelle Porcelli

It has always been a touchy subject, my hands. Even as an elementary school child I would get relentlessly teased about my freckles and extremely pale appearance. The skin on my hands appeared so translucent that my veins looked mostly like a road map, an IV nurse's delight.

Growing up, I learned to ignore the taunts and to cherish the many functions my hands could perform. So, the day I thought I might have lost permanent function was the beginning of a very humbling experience. Although what I went through may be small in comparison to others trials, it is the struggle I faced. And, it is the struggle I continue to face, but this time I choose to go through this with Him, together . . .

Thursday

A halting gasp escaped my breath as the fireworks of pin-prick became unbearable. The sensation swirled around all ten fingers and then surged to both hands. I shot straight up in bed and looked at the clock.

1:30AM

My exhausted body was forced awake as the numbness robbed me of rational thought. What was happening to me? I wondered if I was dreaming as I noticed the tree shadows moving on my wall. Then I heard the wind crash and the sound jolted my body and the shivers of stress overtook me. My thoughts raced as my heart began to flutter and I tried to make sense of what was going on.

I reached to turn on my table lamp and realized I couldn't open either hand to twist the small knob. I rolled out of bed and nudged the overhead light switch with my shoulder and then looked down to see my hands. I discovered they both were curled into fists so tight my veins bulged. My mind became paralyzed with fear. I could feel the pain and tingling of sharp needles engulfing my hands but couldn't open my fingers. It was the same sensation that occurs when my foot fall asleep, except it was both sets of hands, including palms and fingers, and I couldn't move them to get blood circulation going and attempt to wake them up.

The panic grew and I woke up my sweet husband while shrieking, "I need to go to the emergency room. Now!" Dean quickly shuffled awake, we both changed into some sweats, and headed to the hospital.

I was horrified by thoughts of what could be happening. My mind raced through scenarios. I must have diabetes like my father, arthritis like my mother, MS like Aunt Fae, Lupus like my friend Jane, and any other thought that had the potential to catastrophize the situation.

I had no intention of praying or asking God for insight. In my panic, I did the exact opposite. My heart began to harden and I was getting angry. Being scared, angry, and in pain is not a good combination. Those three emotions can do interesting things to your mind. I was angry He would let this happen to me when I had tried to be such a faithful servant.

My thoughts demanded that bad things shouldn't happen to people like me. I went to church. I said my prayers, periodically at least. I said yes to callings. I was a good ministering sister. What happened? Was I forgotten?

The emergency room doctors ran test after test, blood work, glucose panels, and still came up with empty answers. They didn't know what was happening. They couldn't explain how these symptoms spread to both hands at the exact same time. No one could. They suggested it was stress or an emotional issue. Really? I woke up from a dead sleep in agonizing pain and the only answer was stress? Expert let down number one.

I was sent home defeated but knew I had no other option than to push through the day, hopeful after a good night's rest I would wake up to find everything all better.

Friday

The next morning was even worse. The pain wasn't as severe, but that was because my fingers were now becoming so numb and immobile I was worried I would lose all function permanently. At this point I was scrambling for my own answers and found an online ad for a clinic where they send electrical impulses throughout your hands to stimulate nerve growth. I had to give it a shot.

The clinic tried three times to push an IV needle into my arms to issue vitamin B12. Unfortunately, I was so dehydrated my veins didn't play nice and they gave up. They then wrapped electrodes around my wrists resulting in jolts and shocks dancing throughout my hands. I was hopeful. They were hopeful. I could feel nerves being stimulated which was a good sign I had sensation for a moment. Then, once they took the wraps off, most of the numbness returned and the outcome was that there was no significant improvement. In fact, my hands felt worse with more sharp pin pricks in some fingers, numbness in others and more pain everywhere. Expert let down number two.

Just then they wheeled in a man who is a quadriplegic. He was also getting treatment. They placed him right across from me. I watched as his wife took off his shoes and placed his feet back onto the wheelchair. He wasn't complaining, but seemed excited, hopeful that he might get some nerve regeneration. It was a bit of a wake up call to me. Yes, I was in pain, but the rest of my body was functioning just fine. I could have rejoiced in what I had, like my friend who rejoiced in what he hoped he would have.

Throughout all of this the one digit that didn't seem affected and worked quite well were my thumbs. My glorious thumbs! This means I could still pick things up but couldn't do small tactile things like hold a pen. Twisting off a lid from a soda bottle was unheard of. I grieved over that fact for sure!

I got pretty good at using my new Lego-Woman hands, notoriously named so by my daughter, Taylor; which sounds funny now, but at the time it wasn't a joke. I could still drive and tightly twist my fingers around the steering column as long as I turned on the hand heater. The steering wheel would get extremely hot, but the hotter it was the better my hands felt. This heat would eventually be a clue about what was ultimately happening regarding the inflammation in my hands.

Tuesday

I went to an endocrinologist for even more panel testing. I told him I felt like others were beginning to second guess my pain or condition as if it was all in my head. I appreciated how kind he was and he acknowledged my pain was real and did not treat me like I was crazy. However, upon receiving the results, you guessed it, test after test they found nothing. Expert let down number three.

The Following Thursday—One Week Enduring

I was hopeful to get an appointment with a renowned hand surgeon who specializes in carpal tunnel issues. That had to be the ultimate answer, right? Nope. I waited two hours in the office before I needed to be back to work and never even saw that doctor. Expert let down number four.

I was still learning how to function and ironically, could still use a laptop as fingers are curved when typing. Although I looked interesting while doing so, that was a blessing so I could still function at work.

Two Weeks Enduring

I was then referred to have a nerve conduction study done. Sounds fun, right? During this procedure they stick electrodes under your skin and while you are bleeding all over yourself, they shock the heck out of you to check your nerve function. The specialist found, 'nothing wrong with the left hand and only 'slight' carpal tunnel in the right hand.' Expert let down number five.

After two weeks, my fingers weren't as tense as they were in the beginning. I had discovered that running them under very hot water helped them to relax and feel a little better. So from time to time, I would turn on the hot water and let the heat run over my hands until they felt better and started to open up again. Once I turned off the water and my hands cooled, they would curl up again. Noticing this patter, I decided to try purchasing some heated fingerless gloves. I guessed that the issue wasn't really my fingers but my joints and tendons. The gloves were a huge blessing and I also looked pretty cool wearing them. I had to find laughter and solace in something, right?

Three Weeks Enduring

When I went to work the first morning I had my gloves, I wondered what reason I should give my students for my wearing black gloves. They notice everything, even if you part your hair differently. I was already a hot commodity as a Lego woman and didn't want to cause more distraction or make them sad that I didn't have that persona anymore. However, another student gave me the most fabulous answer . . .

"Are you dressed up like Black Widow?" one of my students hopefully questioned.

"No, but I do think she's pretty cool."

"Oh," they responded, "Me too."

And that was that.

The gloves forced my fingers open just a bit, which was a huge blessing and by this point I could pick things up with my thumbs and my pointer finger pretty well. I still couldn't untwist a Diet Dr. Pepper soda bottle lid so that would explain at least some of my orneriness.

Despite the small improvements, my mental health was tanking. I remember thinking, "This is my new life now. I have been through so many tests, needles, IV treatments. It just isn't worth it. I feel like surrendering and giving up."

I have learned that when we are in the frame of mind of, "It's not worth it. I give up," that life can go many different directions. If we feed into the negativity our physical and mental health will also respond negatively and spiral downward. If we face challenges head on, never giving up on ourselves nor giving up on the Savior, we may not be released from the pain or struggles, but somehow they seem more manageable. We realize we are not alone and that He has been there all along.

Four Weeks Enduring

One morning I felt inspired to go back to the hand surgeon. You know, the one I never saw because "I" timed out? Truly, I think I was more offended that they made me wait so long in that hard chair for two hours with no communication. I let my being offended get in the way of what potentially could have been just what I needed. But, I knew I had to give it one more shot at figuring this out.

An entire month had passed since that first night I woke up in pain by this point and my fingers were opening up even more, although still with tingling nerves prickling over the fingers. But, I was glad I could move my hand better.

At the hand surgeon's office the doctor was too busy to see me (of course!), so I saw the nurse practitioner. After talking with me and going over all my previous health tests she exclaimed, "I really don't know what is wrong. We can't figure it out. We can do carpal tunnel surgery on the right hand to see if it will help, but that is doubtful. The fact your hands are always cold and that extreme heat feels good tells me it isn't a carpal tunnel situation." Expert let down number six.

I was devastated and doubted my own inspiration. When that happens my mind plays tricks on me and I begin to doubt every inspired moment I have ever had. But, I have found that if I can hold on just a little bit longer, I will often see where God has His hand in the details, including whom I need in my life at specific moments.

Just as she was leaving the office, she abruptly had a thought enter her mind. She looked at me very puzzled and asked, "Are you Scandinavian?" I responded, "Yes, my grandmother was full Swedish."

She then requested, "Let me look at your palms." She examined my fingers and noticed the puckering around each of my joints. She then revealed, "I think you have Dupuytren Contracture!"

"Dupu what?" I responded, puzzled and curious.

Thank heavens she let me know, "There is another name for it, Viking Syndrome."

Dupuytren permanently bends fingers into a fixed position, it can become difficult to grasp large objects or make simple movements like twisting a lid seem impossible. The thumb and index finger aren't usually affected. It is more common in people with Nordic or Scandinavian ancestry.

After she revealed her discovery to me I asked, "So what can I do about it?"

I kid you not, this was her response to my question, "There is no cure but there are treatments. I don't think we do anything until your hand is completely immobilized. You will just have to fight it."

What? I have to fight it? I didn't know if I should be offended, brave, or just cry. She didn't even give me a chance to ask the two-thousand questions in my mind but rather gave me advice on mental health, managing stress, and so on.

I remember thinking, "Doesn't she know who I am? I teach OTHERS how to manage stress. I don't have that type of problem here."

However, a spiritual feeling came over my body that merely said, "BE STILL."

I have never been 'still' in my entire life, how could I do that now?

Then, a calm feeling entered my body and impressed on my mind were the thoughts, "Be still and know that I am God. I am here. We have got this."

Wow! "WE" was such a magical word to hold in my mind. I let down my pride and realized I would simply have to trust the Lord had sent me at this time, to this place, to be assigned nurse practitioner, to hear her insight and ideas about a diagnosis, so she could tell me, "You just have to fight this."

Instead of being offended, I was relieved. I wasn't scared anymore. My mind and body were still, but now I held a soothing energy encouraging me to 'fight this.' Mentally, it was the best thing for me to know I was in control again, that I held the power to unite with God, and together WE would fight this.

Later that night, my husband in his 'gentle' ways suggested I force my fingers open. I laughed so hard and didn't know if I wanted to slug him or kiss him. So, I did both! (TMI?) Once I slowly forced each finger open the feeling in my fingers slowly started to come back with blood circulation improving. It was so painful, but I knew if I could make it through the pain, the healing would be worth it.

A Child Shall Lead Them

The day my hands were paralyzed was a curse, but it was also a blessing. I had been struggling with feelings of anger and pity and wondering what the point of all this suffering was about. What could possibly happen to turn all that around?

After forcing my fingers open and realizing I really could manage this, at least at some level, I went to work trying to have a better attitude and controlling my feelings of self pity.

I work at a title one elementary school as a counselor and it is hard. Really hard. However, on many occasions I have learned so much about the power of God and how He is mindful of all of His children.

The day after my husband suggested I force my hands open, a student was late coming to school and really struggled entering the classroom. She was crying in the hallway and just outside my door, so I went to see what the problem was. The secretary pulled me aside to let me know she had just witnessed her dog being hit by a car, but her parents both worked and needed her to be at school that day.

"I see," I responded and received instant insight on what to do next.

I knelt down beside her and told her it was okay to cry and that we could cry together.

I sat down next to her, and we both sat in the hallway, crying, calming, being still.

I then asked her if she would like to come to my room to talk about it. She didn't say a word to me. She just looked at me with her big beautiful eyes. She then shook her head to say yes, stood up, and while I was still sitting on the ground, she reached her hand out to me to help ME up. She was so little but had a huge heart.

I took her hand and stood up the best I could without really pulling on her. She wanted to hold hands as we walked around the corner and into my classroom. She began to hum a song and swing our hands a bit. She even giggled when I started humming back.

I couldn't have done this just the day before with my hand. I couldn't have done it a week or even two weeks before. But, I could do it on this day for this little girl, this child of God. I knew that it wasn't a coincidence. God is mindful of all His children and cares enough about each one of us no matter how big or small our struggles may seem.

Today, this student regularly checks in with me and waves as she walks by, and I can now wave back with a friendly open hand. Sometimes it still hurts and I am in pain, but when I see these kids the pain seems to lessen and my worries don't seem so big.

I am blessed.

Viking syndrome has definitely been a tool to humble me. Because of it, I have reached out in prayer more than ever in my life. When all the other experts, although well meaning, had let me down, I decided to turn to the one expert I knew would never let me down. Even if it took me a while to see that.

Heavenly Father knew I needed a humble heart to become vulnerable to His will. He also blessed me with a fighting spirit to overcome physical and mental difficulties. I will likely struggle with this syndrome my entire life, but for now I can open my hands, use them to perform daily tasks and can even play pickleball again!

Sure, I wake up a few times every night to find my hands are in the shape of a Lego-fist again. However, I know those middle of the night "wake-ups" are God winks to remind me to stretch my fingers. I have to stretch my fingers multiple times a day as well likely, for the rest of my life. But that's okay. We have got this, together.

The Living Atonement

Physical and mental ailments go hand in hand. The psychosomatic connection is so powerful. It is wonderful to think that Christ loved us so much He not only gave His physical life for us, but He suffered mentally, emotionally, and even spiritually. Every doubt you or I have right now or in the past, He understands. That is what the Garden of Gethsemane was all about. It was Him experiencing every heartache, sorrow, grief and even joy that we may experience during earth life.

If you ever doubt staying in the gospel will be worth it, if you ever doubt being a faithful member will be worth it, if you ever doubt the physical, emotional, or spiritual struggles will be worth it . . . look to Him. He felt that too, and He overcame everything. You too can overcome.

The greatest joy of Jesus's ministry was even more profound than healing someone or even bringing someone back from the dead. The greatest joy that Jesus brought was when he saved people from their sin!

He focused on the joy we would feel when we repent, the joy we feel when we think of His sacrifice, the joy we feel when we know we can return to our Father in Heaven.

It wasn't nails that kept Jesus on the cross. It was His love. It was His joy, joy for you, joy for me, joy that our burdens may become light, joy that sins can be forgiven, joy that we can return again to paradise.

He lived to die and died to live again. And because He lives again, there is hope. There is joy.

There is no bit of pain or sorrow you are experiencing now that He hasn't already felt deeply and ultimately.

Be still and turn to Him, in joy.

You have got this.

We have got this,

Together.

XV

Healing the World One Heart at a Time

By Thomas Ballard

In 2018, I lived on the Washington coast. I was an emergency substitute Spanish teacher by day, a beachcomber by late afternoon, and an amateur rock carver by night. Each day I would teach, then jog down the beach to my favorite rockhounding spot and search for agates and pretty pebbles. I'd skip rocks for hours, watch the herons and otters, and then jog home with my pockets full of beautiful rocks.

After dinner, I'd take my rock saw (a yard sale find) and cut open the rocks I'd brought home. I loved the moment when the rocks I cut would fall open and reveal their inner colors and patterns—I still do. God is such an artist, and He loves colors.

During that time, I used my daily jogs, rock collecting, and rock carving as self-therapy. I hadn't been diagnosed with bipolar disorder yet, but that didn't change the fact that I was very much in the throes of mania and crippling depression. I was doing my best to be my very best self, yet I was experiencing extreme bouts of depression and thoughts of self-harm. Sometimes I wished that I could just blink out of existence.

The hardest part was when a thought—for example, "My family would be better off without me"—would enter my mind uninvited, then come around over and over like a revolving door, filling every free moment, corroding my heart bit by bit until I more than believed it. After a while, I longed to blink out of existence.

These dark days turned into weeks of missed work. I'd get up early to begin getting ready for work, only to have hours-long panic attacks and call in sick last minute. I used up my sick days and vacation days and dipped into unpaid leave. I wanted to work—I longed for human connection, for purpose—but instead, I'd pass the whole morning huddled by my space heater, in the fetal position, weeping like there was a never-ending flow of sorrow seeping from my bones.

One particularly dark rainy day, I was jogging down the beach. I couldn't breathe. My thoughts were so dark and intense that my body seemed to be shutting down. Between labored, heaving, broken, shallow, gasping breaths, I prayed out loud, as best as I could. My mind was outrunning me, shouting at me to cease existing. I fell to the ground, ready to be done. That's when I found a little half-dollar-sized white quartz rock, ocean-tumbled for millennia, waiting right then and there for me. I scooped it up and took a look, then held it to my mouth and blew off the clinging wet sand. That's when I really saw the rock—it was a heart shape. After months of collecting thousands of rocks off that very beach, I knew at that moment that finding that white, heart-shaped rock was God's way of saying to me, "Tom, I care."

I kept that rock in my pocket for many dark days. Weeks even. Some days it was my reminder that I matter. Others, that I am a good person. Others, that my family loves me, and that God loves me.

I noticed that the heart rock was my constant reminder of truth, and the reminder message it gave shifted to be what I needed when I needed it, kind of like a little Liahona.

I fell in love with the idea that my little heart rock was so meaningful to me. I wondered if a heart rock could be meaningful for others, so I returned to the beach and began collecting naturally shaped heart rocks.

When I'd hear that someone in the community was going through their own rough time, I'd give them a little naturally shaped heart rock and say something like, "When life is really hard, feel your heart rock, and it'll remind you that you matter, you're loved, and you're not alone."

The more I looked outward and reached out to others, the less inwardly trapped I felt.

I did some research and discovered that this powerful concept of transforming objects into reminders has a name. In psychology they call it "creating an artifact." What happens is that your act of giving a personalized message with the physical object triggers the recipient's memory to recall the message each time they see and handle the physical item. Otherwise, the brain would see the object and only recognize it as an object. You can literally do it with any item. (In fact, you do it all the time when you write and give someone a thoughtful, handwritten note.)

I discovered that having heart rocks on hand not only reminded me of truths but also reminded me to look out for others. This changed my perspective, slowly evolving it from a very self-aware, self-critical, self-deprecating one to a more open-minded, thoughtful, hopeful, and charitable one. I liked the way I was feeling, so I collected more heart rocks.

I began keeping heart rocks in my pocket, backpack, and car cup holder. I began hiding them in public places, giving them to the school counselor to hand out, and every so often, I'd give heart rocks to people I knew were going through rough experiences.

I felt like every heart rock I gave away helped me become a kind person. It was the kind of person I wanted to become. So naturally, I decided to give away a lot of heart rocks.

Eventually, naturally shaped heart rocks became scarce on my favorite jogging beaches. While on an unsuccessful heart-rock hunting jog, I had a brilliant idea: "If the ocean can make a heart rock, why can't I?" I visualized myself taking the rock slabs I had been making during my numerous evening rock-cutting sessions and shaping them into hearts. I ran home and did just that: I made my first beautiful, wonky heart rocks.

The very next day at school, I had the perfect opportunity to give them away. As I recalled my experiences giving away the heart rocks, I realized that I had felt the Holy Ghost testify to me that the truths I shared with the people I gave my heart rocks to were also true for me. I realized that they matter, they are loved, they are beautiful, they are not alone, and so am I—I matter, I am loved, I am beautiful, and I am not alone. I recognized how dramatically different I was feeling, and I determined to make more heart rocks—a lot of heart rocks.

I bought a larger rock saw and made hundreds of little heart rocks.

I gave them away one at a time.

I had many wonderful experiences.

I was still living with undiagnosed bipolar disorder, and it was getting progressively worse—I was just unwittingly coping with it much better.

Collecting pretty rocks to make into hearts was a fun treasure hunt and something for me to look forward to each day—even on Washington's famous rainy, dark days.

Cutting the rocks was my art therapy. Creating something with my hands always felt incredibly rewarding.

Having heart rocks with me at all times reminded me of the truths I needed to remember and reminded me that I'm not alone in my difficulties and that I should notice others and be kind to them.

Handing out heart rocks to others became easier for me. It felt natural. It felt like giving out the rocks to help lift others' spirits was part of my life purpose. I felt like I was becoming "Tom, the Heart Rock Guy," and I began to see myself that way.

One heart rock at a time, I was deepening my friendships, helping others cope with their own difficulties, and creating opportunities for the Holy Ghost to testify of truths.

I felt like I had a purpose, and it was exciting! So much good was happening!

Then, on Thanksgiving 2019, my brother-in-law ended his life.

* * *

I was devastated, shaken to the core.

I tried to drive home to Utah to be with family and to attend the funeral, but there was a blizzard and I couldn't make it through the mountain pass. I had to turn around.

I've never felt so alone.

Chapter xv: Healing the World One Heart at a Time

I made heart rocks all night. I made them for my widowed sister and her young daughters. I made a heart rock for my brother-in-law. I made a heart rock for myself.

Losing a loved one to suicide was as shocking as it was painful!

I swore in my immense grief that I would use my life to do whatever I could to prevent a death by suicide—I didn't want other people, other families, to feel the horrible pain that I was feeling.

For weeks all I could think about was the pain of what felt like an unnecessary loss. I wanted to do something! I thought about the impact that a few hundred heart rocks had made in my little remote community. I wondered, "What would happen if I made and gave away 100,000 heart rocks? Could they potentially be used to save a life by preventing a death by suicide? Could I get other caring individuals to help me give heart rocks to the people who need them the most?"

I bought a bigger rock saw and began making hundreds of heart rocks each week. I gave them away as fast as I was able to make them.

I ended the school year and then came a big surprise; my widowed sister called me and asked me to move back to Utah to help support her and her daughters. So I did.

I loaded a moving truck with thirty, five-gallon buckets of rocks, and I drove the 880 miles home to Utah. I set up my "Rock Carving Studio" in the unfinished basement, and whenever I needed to be applying for jobs, I would instead go make heart rocks. (It was a lot more fun!)

I learned that several local schools had lost students to suicide. I did some research and was floored when I found out how many local students, kids even, had ended their lives. I realized that I could do something about it. So I did. Instead of spending entire days writing resumes and cover letters and applying to jobs I had zero interest in taking, I decided to live on my savings for a few months and flood local schools with heart rocks. I began making and distributing a hundred heart rocks every day.

My sister had a great recommendation: that I try having a booth selling heart rocks at a farmers' market. She said it would be a good way for me to share my message about using heart rocks to spread kindness and save lives with a lot of people, and to potentially do some fundraising and networking too. I took her advice, and with a lot of help from my family, I did my first market.

At the market, I spoke with several hundred people about the heart rocks, sold forty-five of them, and gave away fifty more. After paying my booth fee, I made $225. I considered it a resounding success!

I began working at six markets a week, and when I wasn't at markets, I was making heart rocks.

At most markets, I'd give away heart rocks as often as I felt impressed to, and I felt impressed to a lot. Sometimes when I was having a particularly difficult day, I'd give a heart rock to people as they walked by. Often at markets, I'd give away hundreds of free heart rocks. It wasn't always a good way to make money, but it was an incredible way to lift my spirits and have a positive impact on others around me.

At the farmers' markets, I began meeting school administrators, school counselors, teachers, therapists, youth group leaders, concerned parents, nurses, and others who were very interested in flooding their families, schools, communities, and organizations with heart rocks.

Eventually, I came up with the policy that for every heart rock I sold, I would also donate one to a school counselor or local therapist to use as a tool for suicide prevention.

Suddenly I had a means to fund making heart rocks and a great way to network, finding individuals to distribute the heart rocks one by one.

* * *

While doing a weekly farmers' market, I met a woman who told me she had lost several family members to suicide and was also struggling with, well, a lot. I offered her ten heart rocks and said, "You're not the only one feeling this way. Find the others and give them heart rock reminders. Then next week come tell me about your experience, and I'll give you more rocks."

The next week I gave her another twenty heart rocks.

The next week forty.

Then the next week she came in tears because she had lost another loved one to suicide. She invited me to come to the funeral and asked if she could have seventy-six heart rocks. I was surprised by the very

Chapter XV: Healing the World One Heart at a Time

specific number. She explained that she would have seventy-six family members at the funeral, and she wanted to offer each of them a heart rock. I agreed.

Later that week at the funeral service, I sat near the door and watched her hand out seventy-six heart rocks, one at a time, to every member of her family. She explained the meaning of the heart rock to each family member and invited them to choose their favorite heart rock. While they were selecting their heart rock, she told them exactly what she wanted it to remind them of. Each family member received a unique heart rock and a unique, heartfelt message with it. She told each of them, "When you're having one of those dark, awful days that we all get, I want you to find your heart rock and hold it. It will remind you that . . ."

I was touched by her kindness. We said our goodbyes and agreed to meet at next week's farmers' market.

A week rolled by, the farmers' market came and went, and I didn't see her. Another week, another market, and still she didn't show.

A few days later, my mom called me and told me to come get my geodes out of her flowerbed. I'd completely forgotten about them and was excited to see if I could make them into hearts. I spent the evening doing a very special heart rock carving session. At 11 p.m., when I finished, I wanted to text my mom pictures of the beautiful hearts that I had made. (I have a character flaw: I love to be a showoff and receive praise.) Only I knew it was too late and she'd be asleep. I thought about who I could show the geode heart rocks to, and I remembered my friend from the farmers' market. I didn't have her phone number, but I had recently started using Instagram and realized I could message her there.

I pulled out my phone, snapped a few photos of the geode hearts, found her Instagram profile, and sent her the pictures of the hearts, saying, "Hey _____, I just made these beautiful geode heart rocks. I think they're the most beautiful hearts I've ever made. They reminded me of your beautiful heart. I'm glad we're friends and hope that every time you see your heart rocks, they remind you that this world is a better place because you are in it."

I sent it and began cleaning up. A couple of minutes later she responded, and it caught me completely off guard. She said that at that very moment, she was contemplating ending her life and had the means to do it. She said she saw my message and picked up her heart rock, and it immediately changed the way she was feeling. She messaged me saying she still felt terribly and didn't know what to do. We talked about feelings and heart rocks. Then I offered to bring her some food and passed along the Suicide Prevention Hotline number. She said, "Thanks, but no thanks," to my offer for some food, but she graciously accepted my invitation to call the Suicide Prevention Hotline. After calling it, she began receiving professional help and continued getting and distributing her weekly supply of farmers' market heart rocks.

Although it has been several years and I no longer do that particular farmers' market, we're still in touch, she is doing much better, and she still treasures her heart rock reminder. She keeps it close, and on particularly difficult days, she keeps it in her pocket where she can always reach it.

I mention this story because it was the first time I ever realized that one of my heart rocks may have saved a life.

* * *

About that same time, I began getting invited to speak to youth groups, at community events, and even at school assemblies. I began sharing my unique story about using heart rock reminders to help others and using kindness to deepen friendships, strengthen family ties, and maybe even save lives.

I met with a student council and gave each member three heart rocks. I told them to keep one as their reminder that they matter, are loved, and are not alone. I instructed them to keep the other two hearts with them until they found the right moment to give them away.

Four months later, one of those students shared with me on Instagram that they had kept their third heart rock in their pocket for four months before finally finding someone who needed it. They shared their incredible experience and said they felt like they had successfully used their heart rock to prevent a peer from ending their life.

Chapter xv: Healing the World One Heart at a Time

By this time, I had hand-carved and distributed over 17,000 heart rocks. More importantly, I realized that my efforts to spread kindness and love *had* made a difference, *especially* for those two individuals.

But then I discovered a problem—a big problem. I had made so many heart rocks and made them so frequently that I started ruining my hands from all of the cold water, vibration, and repetitive motion. I sometimes would even wake up and find that I had been holding my hands and arms in a carving position while I slept. I knew I needed to find help keeping up with the carving, but I didn't know what to do. So I did something; I prayed.

I felt so silly praying and fasting about making and distributing heart rocks. However, I do feel like I received guidance. I had a recurring thought: "Think bigger. Think bigger." And, well, I've tried.

Within days of that initial prayer, I had a weird message on my social media. It was a stone carver, about my same age, messaging me from the other side of the planet, offering to help me make heart rocks. We used a lot of Google Translate and pictures to reach a mutually beneficial agreement. (Actually, we were both thrilled about it and still are!) I offer guaranteed monthly income to make heart rocks for kids in Utah schools, and their help making the hearts has freed me up to focus on distributing them. (When I needed more heart rocks, I hired his brother, his many cousins, his neighbors, his friends, and so on. I now have dozens of families helping me make many thousands of heart rocks each month and hundreds more on a wait-list.)

Don't get me wrong, I still carve many heart rocks. But now I mainly make heart rocks for my own creative therapy and always just to give away.

Around the same time I started collaborating with the stone carver, I began to realize that I could use social media to effectively distribute heart rocks. I began creating digital content and slowly grew a very supportive organic following of people who love what I do and want to help me flood the world with heart rock reminders.

One day, one of my Instagram followers messaged me saying that they had just lost a family member to suicide. They said they wished they had had a heart rock last week to give to them.

This experience brought back in full strength the pain I had felt when I lost my brother-in-law to suicide. It almost felt like I was reliving the pain. I decided to do something drastic to get more heart rocks to the people who need them the most.

So I began using my social media and website to offer free heart rocks to be used as tools for people currently experiencing thoughts of self-harm or suicide. Within months, I shipped hundreds of the rocks and handwritten notes to complete strangers.

Then I expanded the offer of free heart rocks to anyone who *knows* someone who may be experiencing thoughts of self-harm or suicide and promises to use the free heart rock reminders as tools for suicide prevention. Within several months, I shipped over a thousand heart rocks to individuals who either were experiencing suicidal ideation or knew someone who was.

I now have heart rocks in all fifty states and in over fifty-five countries reminding people that they matter, they are loved, and they are not alone.

On May 24, 2022, I heard the news about the school shooting tragedy in Uvalde, Texas, and I realized I could do something to help. So I did. I spent months making thousands of heart rocks and then drove twenty-six hours to get there. (I could only bring 8,000 heart rocks because any more would have bottomed-out my Prius . . .) I distributed the heart rocks one at a time through all of the churches, schools, counseling centers, emergency service providers, mortuaries, nursing and retirement homes, public libraries, and many of the local businesses.

A year later, in September 2023, I visited Uvalde a second time. (This time I flew with some of the heaviest luggage to pass through the SLC airport!) With the help of Uvalde's incredible residents, I was able to distribute another 7,500 heart rocks. It was an incredible experience! (There are now officially more heart rocks than people in Uvalde, and I plan to return yearly to distribute more.)

As of January 2024, I have been able to distribute over 200,000 heart rocks. I've personally handed out 70,000 of them, but the rest have been distributed by wonderful individuals who have used the heart rocks to spread love and kindness in their schools, families, and communities.

Chapter xv: Healing the World One Heart at a Time

Through my social media, I am aware of over one hundred instances where people have successfully used my heart rocks to help prevent potential deaths by suicide.

I've received hundreds of more stories from people sharing how they're using their heart rocks as personal reminders that they matter, sharing them with others to reconnect with estranged family and friends, save lives, and do *so much more*!

I've funded it by being a vendor at over 300 farmers' markets, pop-up markets, and community events. I estimate that I've easily spoken in person to over 250,000 people about using heart rock reminders and kindness to save lives, and I've connected with many more people through my social media reach.

I've done dozens of school assemblies and flooded each of those schools with more heart rocks than students. I invite them to keep their heart rock for as long as they need a reminder that they matter, are loved, and are not alone, and then when they are ready, to pass it on. I also leave hundreds of extra heart rocks accessible to them in their counseling center. Through this effort alone, I'm aware of dozens of instances where students, teachers, and school counselors have used heart rock reminders to directly intervene and prevent potential deaths by suicide. In fact, none of those schools, nor their surrounding communities, have had a death by suicide since being flooded with heart rocks.

People have started calling me "Tom, the Heart Rock Guy," and I love it! But I don't love it for the reasons you might think.

I love it because each day I feel like I have a sense of purpose.

I love the opportunities to spread kindness that I've created for myself, one heart rock at a time. And I love that it's just that simple: one heart rock at a time. It doesn't have to be overwhelming because I'm still doing what I've done all along: taking one heart rock and trying to find someone who needs it more than I do. Then another heart rock and another person.

Every time I make an effort to spread kindness, I feel the power of the Holy Ghost magnify the message for the heart rock recipient *and* for me.

Often I feel the Holy Ghost lead me to people who desperately need heart rock reminders.

Often I feel the Holy Ghost put words in my mouth because God knows His children and knows exactly what they need to hear.

You can do what I'm doing: spread kindness one object to one person, one at a time, and repeat.

You will be guided by the Holy Ghost.

You will be inspired.

You are a more powerful of an influence for good than you could ever imagine!

As you create kindness and give it away one person at a time, God, our Heavenly Father, who knows you *so well*, will slip a little reminder into your hand when you need it the most. As you love His children, you'll feel His love flow through you like a flood.

Your perspective will change as your heart changes from being self-centered to others-centered.

Will life get easier? Well, yes and no. I still live with bipolar disorder and sometimes it's incredibly difficult. On the darkest days I make sure I hand out the most heart rocks. It reminds me that I'm not the only one feeling this way, that I matter, and that I'm loved, seen, wanted, appreciated, beautiful, strong, important, and so on. It invites meaningful human connection, and it invites the Holy Ghost to bear witness of the truths shared.

This all started in a really dark place. And while I still have hard days, dark days, I find so much joy in the purpose I feel I have. I find so much joy in sharing love and kindness. Kindness is a circle, and what I send out always comes back in unexpected ways. My hard times have become my encouragement to help other, and because of that I've found so much that I never thought I would have.

My goal is to give away one more heart rock *and* to distribute one million heart rocks by Thanksgiving 2029.

What's yours?

XVI
Are You Still All In?
By Ganel-Lyn Condie

"Are you still all in with the church?"

A variety of people have asked me multiple times, especially over the past few years, if I'm still "all in." It's a valid question with a complex answer, and it's a conversation worth having. Each time that I have held space for others to share their own questions and struggles regarding faith and religion, I have felt drawn to look at my own reasons for staying.

I have taught my children that conversion is not a one-day decision or a one-moment experience. It's a process of choosing every day to nurture a relationship with God, keep covenants, and continue believing. When I look back on my own conversion path, I see a million moments of choosing.

The short answer is "Yes, I *am* still all in." But here's the longer answer.

In the Beginning

Because you and I are here, we know that we chose to come to earth, receive a body, and have a mortal experience. We don't know a lot about our premortal family home evenings or Sunday School classes, but we do know that we were schooled and prepared to continue forward on the covenant path. "We all shouted for joy in our premortal life when we heard God's plan of happiness, and we continue to shout for joy here as we live according to His plan."[57] Some of God's children were born in the covenant, and others have found or are still searching for it.

I was born into a family of faith. My parents were married in the temple but eventually divorced. At the age of eight, I chose to be baptized by my stepfather, Jim, and confirmed by my father, Dan. I had to be baptized three times because my foot kept popping out of the water. I still remember how I felt that day. I remember the peace of the Spirit. I remember my mom singing "Joseph Smith's First Prayer": "Oh, how lovely was the morning! / Radiant beamed the sun above. . . . When within the shady woodland / Joseph sought the God of love."[58] These words beautifully described the pure and simple faith I had as a child.

It has been forty-five years since my baptism day and my first experience with making a covenant with the Lord. When I reflect on what I felt in 1978, I see it was then that I began to understand the importance of belief and the greater value of *remembering* spiritual experiences. Each time I stood to bear testimony, or when my fervent childhood prayers were answered, I remember again feeling the Spirit I had felt at my baptism. Like that one time I lost a favorite necklace in some backyard ivy—I prayed to find it, and as soon as I said "amen" and stood up, I found it tucked behind a leaf. Sometimes my childhood prayers weren't answered so immediately or directly as finding a lost treasure, but I began to understand how the Spirit spoke to me. He was like a new friend I was just getting to know.

No matter what those first faith encounters are, our conversion path may begin with stepping on simple spiritual stones. But the process of deepening our faith can't stop there. This is just the beginning of consistently choosing to stay on the covenant path, step by step.

---

57. Kevin R. Duncan, "A Voice of Gladness!," *Liahona*, May 2023, 95.
58. "Joseph Smith's First Prayer," *Hymns*, The Church of Jesus Christ of Latter-day Saints, Salt Lake City, UT, no. 26, Gospel Library App.

Chapter XVI: Are You Still All In?

In the Middle

You know when you watch a great movie or read an inspiring book and things get complicated or difficult in the middle of the story? The hero is facing opposition that seems insurmountable. The audience knows that in the end, everything will be resolved. But in the middle, when the drama happens, viewers are still left wondering how things will play out. In our lives, just like in the movies, this is where the real growth happens. The choices we make in the middle are so important.

Faith is complex. It matures through a natural growth cycle of believing, asking questions, and then moving to a deeper level of belief. The middle years—those that span adolescence through the young adult stage—are filled with big decisions, deep questions, and growth opportunities. I remember as a fourteen-year-old doing work for the dead in the Oakland California Temple. As I sat in God's temple, I began to understand the power of making and keeping covenants. I began to see that sitting in sacred spaces opens you up to receiving sanctification. In the temple chapel, I recall feeling connected with heaven in a way unique to being in the temples of God. The feelings I had in God's house felt starkly different than those felt at home.

It was in those rare moments, traveling six hours round trip to the temple, that I began to see the binding power of being in sacred spaces and choosing to make to keep covenants. Back in the day, if you did baptisms for the dead, you got a little card to bring home as a record of how many people you had done ordinance work for. Each time I rode the bus home, as I looked at that card, I could see with my spiritual eyes a personal heavenly team growing in my corner

During high school, I was one of the few members of the Church in my age group. In many ways, it provided unique opportunities to share my faith with friends—and also wrestle with my own whys for staying all in. I didn't always see myself as a daughter of God. I wasn't a perfect example, and I made a lot of adolescent mistakes. But through this season of life, I learned the power and joy of choosing to repent and try again. I'm not exactly sure why, but through it all, I never lost my faith.

On reflection, I remember the impact of loving Young Women leaders, moments singing in youth choirs, and glimmers into what life could be like if I kept choosing to stay on the covenant path. Even when I sometimes got lost in the mist of making mistakes, I knew that beyond any sins or spiritual questions I had, God had a plan of happiness designed just for me.

While I still had a lot to figure out, I made choices in my young life to stay close to the Lord. Attending seminary helped me deepen my understanding of the character of God and awakened a desire to keep learning more about the scriptures. One key decision came after going to Young Women camp. I came home not wanting to lose the Spirit I had felt during that week, and soon after, I followed a prompting and made an appointment with my bishop to get my patriarchal blessing.

As I received my blessing, I caught a glimpse of eternal perspective—that some of my struggles, pain, and questions were only temporary. I remember crying while the patriarch had his hands on my head. The tears fell because I knew then that God not only loved me deeply, but He also *knew* me. My Heavenly Father saw me. My plan of happiness had not always felt happy—through my parents' divorce, family members' mental health struggles, or the death of my little sister Bonnie—but God was whispering through my patriarchal blessing that healing and miracles were still coming.

Eventually, high school graduation day came. As I crossed the stage to get my diploma, I moved my orange tassel across my graduation cap. I was leaving one growth cycle and entering a weightier one. I knew that the choices I would soon make would impact my future, and some would be of eternal importance.

The first of those choices was leaving home to live in Rexburg, Idaho, to attend Ricks College (BYU–Idaho) in the fall of 1989. When I reflect on my teen years, I can see it was then that I began to learn that making mistakes and making decisions are both easier when you choose to include God in the middle of all of the messes. I learned the power of joyfully repenting and trying again. Choosing to go to therapy while attending college taught me that asking for help is education. Everyone can benefit from more learning. I realized that because of my choices in 1989, I could find a new way forward and create a life focused on faith, love, and healing. Searching for my own deep roots of conversion in religion classes, and willingly serving in callings in my ward, helped me learn through experience how God speaks to me and what I mean to Him, regardless of my flaws.

The Beginning of the End

College was the beginning of my forever. When my new bishop assigned our apartment to be in the same family home evening group as a young man named Rob, I had no idea what would soon happen on my conversion path. He was fresh home from his mission to Portugal and a bit shy. We were just friends the whole first year of college. It was during our second year at Ricks when Rob became more than just a friend.

We chose to be married in the Portland Temple in June 1991. We made covenants and plans. I remember, just like on my baptism day, feeling peace and light. Over the subsequent thirty-two years, we have made many decisions and mistakes. Individually and together, we have learned that by choosing to keep *covenants,* they will keep *you*. I don't have the words to describe how this happens, but I do have thirty-three years of evidence to be a witness of this truth.

Rob and I have had a lot of opportunities to grow in our conversion on the covenant path through difficult stewardships. We went to therapy and had a combination of ten years of infertility, multiple job losses, and thirty years of chronic illness. We have struggled with parenting pain, losses of loved ones, and many more moments of miracles.

When I'm asked the question "Why are you still in?" the simplest answer is that through the up and down seasons of my life, I have come to trust the Lord. When we bind ourselves to God, He will bind us to Him. He has answered so many prayers—not always how and when I thought, but *always.* The Spirit has confirmed the truth to my heart time and time again. As I've put the Lord and His promises to the test, He has never failed me.

The restored gospel of Jesus Christ is the place where my covenants live, so here I too will stay. I testify that what President Russell M. Nelson taught is true: we can "find rest from the intensity, uncertainty, and anguish of this world by overcoming the world through [our] covenants with God."⁵⁹ In the last three decades, through my covenants and choices, my faith has deepened not in spite of the tougher trials I've faced but because of them.

I have gone through times when God has felt very distant. There have been seasons when there were definitely more questions than answers coming. And there have been experiences with other members of my faith who have said and done things that made it really challenging to stay. But all relationships grow when you keep investing in them. As I have made the choice to prioritize and invest in my relationship with God, it continues to grow. Weekly church attendance, temple service, and daily communion in prayer and scripture study haven't stopped the hard from happening, but they have given me access to God's grace to transcend the hard. I don't know how the end of my journey will look or feel, but I am committed to choosing to live "all in" during this time—from now to the very end. As Elder David A. Bednar taught:

> We begin to abide in the Lord by exercising our moral agency to take upon ourselves His yoke through the covenants and ordinances of the restored gospel. The covenant connection we have with our Heavenly Father and His resurrected and living Son is the supernal source of perspective, hope, power, peace, and enduring joy; it also is the rock-solid foundation upon which we should build our lives. We abide in Him by striving continually to strengthen our individual covenant bond with the Father and the Son. For example, praying sincerely to the Eternal Father in the name of His Beloved Son deepens and fortifies our covenant connection with Them.⁶⁰

Conversion is a daily choice. Each day, we have the opportunity to choose to cultivate our conversion by yoking ourselves to Christ. That looks like choosing to remember our early foundational spiritual experiences. It means including God while in the middle of making mistakes and major decisions. It also requires choosing to make and

---

59. Russell M. Nelson, "Overcome the World and Find Rest," *Liahona*, Nov. 2022, 97.
60. David A. Bednar, "Abide in Me, and I in You; Therefore Walk with Me," *Liahona*, May 2023, 124.

keep your covenants so they can keep you—until the end when Jesus comes again.

So that's the long answer. I'm all in! Cultivating my conversion and keeping covenants is complex. But after fifty-two years of life, I look back and testify that it will all be worth it.

XVII
Covenant Power
By Connie Sokol

Years ago, when I was about 12 and living in Oregon, my parents came home one day and said they were no longer going to church. At that age, and as one of the very few Latter-day Saints in the area, my response was, "Sweet!"

But then it hit me—I was about to go into Young Women's (formerly known as Mutual—if you know, you know) and I would not be in the presence of Brandt. He was the Brad Pitt of the very small ward and let's just say, we swooned. In that difficult moment, I realized that our future possible romance was not to be, mourned it, and then thought no more of it.

Fast forward to high school, I was a cheerleader and best friends with a girl named Ann who was of the Lutheran faith. When it came time to decide on a college she chose Pacific Lutheran University—a fabulous school—and invited me to come. We did the school tour; it seemed great, and that became my plan.

Until I happened to meet Brandt.

In Oregon, happening to run into another Latter-day Saint is a miracle in and of itself. But then I experienced what I now call my *jedi moment*. In one of the 600 Star Wars movies, there's a scene where a young Obi-Wan-Kenobi is at a bar and a guy offers him death sticks. Then Obi-Wan waves his hand in an arc and says, "You don't want to sell me death sticks." The man replies with a dazed stare, "I don't want to sell you death sticks." Obi Wan says, "You want to go home and rethink your life." The man says, "I want to go home and rethink my life."

My actual conversation with Brandt went along similar lines (with paraphrasing and inflection freely added).

Brandt: What school are you going to this fall?
Me: Pacific Lutheran University.
Brandt: You don't want to go there (invisible Jedi hand wave).
Me, thoughtfully: I don't want to go there.
Brandt: You want to go to BYU (repeat invisible Jedi hand wave).
Me, nodding: I want to go to BYU.

And I did. That one decision changed the trajectory of my life. Who knew that 40 years later I would be guest teaching and speaking to college students at Brigham Young University, helping them make similar life-changing decisions.

To me, that's the power of covenants. It's being in a moment, a conversation, the throes of a decision, and your soul knows the answer before you cerebrally understand why. I wasn't perfect in my covenant-keeping, but I was doing my best with the knowledge that I had. And though I wasn't sure what BYU even was, my soul felt and knew that's where I needed to be. Covenant power is like a power feed. It's humming all the time, opening you to opportunities, guidance, and solutions beyond your own. In that moment of awareness, you can feel the shift, the something beyond you that buoys needed energy or creates flashes of insight.

That is part of the superpower of covenant living, and it's vital we understand what it is and how to use it.

So What is a Covenant?

Let's get clear about what a covenant is and how it works. President Russell M. Nelson said:

> One of the most important concepts of revealed religion is that of a sacred covenant . . . it is a sacred promise with God . . . When you and I enter that [covenant] path, we have a new way of life. We thereby

create a relationship with God that allows Him to bless and change us. The covenant path leads us back to Him. If we let God prevail in our lives, that covenant will lead us closer and closer to Him.[61]

With that covenant making and keeping now comes access to the Savior's power. President Nelson also said:

> The reward for keeping covenants with God is heavenly power—power that strengthens us to withstand our trials, temptations, and heartaches better. *This power eases our way.* Those who live the higher laws of Jesus Christ have access to His higher power . . . Despite the distractions and distortions that swirl around us, you can find true rest—meaning relief and peace—even amid your most vexing problems.[62]

It is a limitless, never-ending source of spiritual energy, renewal, and enabling power that we can access as needed through the Savior. We can plug into that power every single moment of every single day. Just like plugging in your phone or laptop when we need power, we can plug into that divine Source according to our righteous desires and faith.

So exactly HOW do we plug into and access that power? And then use it, and continue to increase it in our own lives and the lives of others?

Though there are several ways that I've seen, studied, and experienced, I want to focus on three ways we experience His covenant power: Covenant Confidence, Covenant Comfort, and Covenant Capacity.

Christ-centered Covenant Confidence

After my freshman year, I had the privilege to attend BYU-Hawaii. Though I loved the experience, my recurring problem was low funds. But student word got around that the other islands besides Oahu were gorgeous and wouldn't it be awesome to go there? Yes, it

---

61. Russel M. Nelson, *Covenants*, General Conference (Salt Lake City, UT), October 2017, Gospel Library App; italics added.
62. Russel M. Nelson, *Overcome the World and Find Rest*, General Conference (Salt Lake City, UT), October 2022. Gospel Library App; italics added.

would. However, the helicopter flight was out of my financial reach. That's when I heard about two opportunities for performing groups to travel to the islands. Bingo.

Auditions were advertised for the Seaside Singers and the BYU Symphonic Band. I auditioned for the vocal group and luckily was headed to Kauai. Maui remained out of reach.

As I prayed, an idea came. Though it seemed out of reach, I felt a deeper sense in my soul to take the next step, a covenant confidence of not knowing beforehand what the outcome would be, but a willingness to act on what I did know. I went into the office of the band director and sat down across from him. Wearing a tired but kind expression, he asked what I needed. The conversation went something like this:

Me: I would love to audition for the symphonic band.

Him: Terrific. What instrument do you play?

Me: None. [Pause]. But I'm super willing to learn.

Extended pause. Beleaguered slight shake of his head, a possible pleading look to the heavens of 'Give Me Strength.'

Him: Okay.

And I did. I learned how to play the marimba, courtesy of said angel band director (all band directors go to heaven), and went to Maui with the group, where we had a fantastic experience.

Covenant Confidence through Him can do that. It's more than just a good idea and maybe I'll try it. It's a rumble deep in your soul that you know this is the right thing to do, but you just don't know exactly how. This divine Covenant Confidence brings inspiration and innovation to step into who and what you truly can become.

So how do we plug into Covenant Confidence?

First, this divine Covenant Confidence comes from knowing who we REALLY are. President Nelson shared in a Worldwide Devotional for Young Adults:

> I believe that if the Lord were speaking to you directly tonight, the first thing he would make sure you understand is your true identity. My dear friends, you are literally the spirit children of God . . . Second, as a member of the Church, you are a child of the covenant. And third, you are a disciple of Jesus Christ . . .

Tonight, I plead with you not to replace these three paramount and unchanging identifiers with any others, because doing so could stymie your progress or pigeonhole you in a stereotype that could potentially thwart your eternal progression."[63]

Knowing who we truly are generates an internal, divine Covenant Confidence that emanates from us in all we do—how we talk, think, feel, show up, resolve problems, or step into new situations.

Who in the scriptures exudes that kind of confidence?

Mormon staying true amidst war and carnage says, "I am a disciple of Jesus Christ" (3 Nephi 5:13).

Rebekah, asked to leave her family and marry a man she's never met, feels inspired to say, "I will go" (Genesis 24:58).

Deborah, leading the Israelites against the overwhelming Canaanites says, "Up! for this is the day" (Judges 4:14).

Talk about confidence. And we can have that too.

Second, Christ-centered Covenant Confidence comes from making and keeping sacred covenants with our Heavenly Father and the Savior. Learn of Them, read Their words, feel the truths and start living them to your very best. Make and keep the covenants you can, then work toward the ones you have yet to receive. President Nelson stated:

> Your commitment to follow the Savior by making covenants with Him and then keeping those covenants will open the door to every spiritual blessing and privilege available to men, women, and children everywhere.[64]

Experience It

To better understand and strengthen the covenants you've made, try a simple but powerful exercise I like to do with a patriarchal blessing; it's called SIP.

---

63. Russell M. Nelson, Worldwide Devotional for Young Adults at the Conference Center in Salt Lake City, Utah, on May 15, 2022.
64. Russell M. Nelson, "As We Go Forward Together," *Ensign*, Apr. 2018, 7

As you read your patriarchal blessing, look for and highlight three categories: **S**piritual gifts, **I**nstructions, and **P**romises.

After making that list, put it somewhere private but accessible to remind yourself daily of what you already know about who you are and who you can become. For a bonus reminder, each time you sip a drink, think of one of the SIP things you've learned from your blessing. While this is not the 11th commandment, it can be a helpful exercise to get a little more clarity on what the Lord is trying to share with you about you.

Christ-centered Covenant Comfort

After twenty-five years of marriage and raising seven children, I went through a divorce. One day I felt strongly that I needed to attend the temple, but not my usual one. This temple was in Provo, about 30 minutes away. It had been a hard week and my heart and even my limbs felt a bit like Atlas, as if I were perpetually bearing a crushing load.

As I entered the initiatory's area, I was surprised to find there were only three women waiting on the benches. I sat next to the last woman and opened the scriptures. Starting in the Topical Guide, I remember thinking, "I don't want direction today, I just want comfort." For the past months I had been strong, clear-headed, and highly functioning. But today, I was tired and needed a spiritual hug.

I turned to the Comfort category and a scripture reference stood out to me, which read:

"I am he; yea, I am he that *comforteth* you . . ."[65]

Immediately, my eyes teared up and I felt an overwhelming whoosh of love from head to toe. Then I noticed a verse on the opposite page:

> For the Lord shall *comfort* Zion, he will *comfort* all her waste places; and he will make her wilderness like Eden, and her desert like the garden of the Lord. Joy and gladness shall be found therein, thanksgiving and the voice of melody (2 Nephi 8:3, italics added).

---

65. 2 Nephi 8:12; italics added

At that same moment, I felt a soft tap on my knee and looked up. There, inexplicably, was a dear friend of 30 years, looking at me with confused wonder at seeing me in this temple.

I immediately threw my arms around her neck and started sobbing, and she simply held me. In an instant, I knew. I knew that He knew me, that He knew my need to feel that hug, and that tangible comfort from a dear friend who also knew me.

That's Covenant Comfort. It's not choreographing all the needs or feels all on your own. It's the gift of a loving Heavenly Father who, because of your covenant-keeping, can orchestrate so much more on your behalf, just when you need it.

So how do we plug into that kind of divine Covenant Comfort?

One way is to seek for it in the places we can more easily find it—the temple, the scriptures, the prayer places where our hearts are open and ready to receive. It's also finding and practicing healthy, appropriate coping skills and self-care practices that ease the stress and strain of this world. It's actively seeking the Savior in the whole process.

My current stake president, President Darren Averett, shared in our Stake Vision:

> We invite you to develop other geographic places of connection to the Savior (i.e., a room, a chair, a porch, a closet, a car ride with no radio, your commute, a mountain, a walk, etc.) where you can regularly go to separate yourself from distraction and to connect to His power, answers, guidance, healing, and joy.[66]

He also encouraged us to "always have a temple appointment scheduled" and that changed the way I planned my week to include the environment and opportunities to feel His comfort.

This principle of creating ways to feel that comfort applies to school and work situations. At one point I experienced a difficult situation in my business. A variety of shifts all at once washed over me like an unexpected tidal wave. Though I personally hadn't experienced serious anxiety before, in this situation, I suddenly did. For weeks, every

---

66. Darren Averett, Stake Vision, Salem Utah Stake of the Church of Jesus Christ of Latter-day Saints, https://suwhstake.org/salem-utah-woodland-hills-stake-vision/

morning I awoke with a weight on my chest, a feeling of dread and angst that felt like a physical churning.

Even though I was daily doing scripture study, weekly attending the temple and church, and consistently keeping my covenants, nothing shifted. I used several coping skills like breathing, exercising, journaling, etc. I was able to function during the day, but every morning the anxious feeling was back.

Then one day the thought came, "immersion." I saw that word in my scripture study, and I had used it in a previous experience to be successful. The immersion concept was to immerse myself in time, energy, or focus in a spiritual tool to get increased strength, not to an extreme and not to seek some miraculous manifestation. It is simply to reconnect more fully with the divine.

President Spencer W. Kimball shared:

> I find that when I get casual in my relationships with divinity and when it seems that no divine ear is listening and no divine voice is speaking, that I am far, far away. If I immerse myself in the scriptures the distance narrows and the spirituality returns.[67]

So I started "immersion" reading the Book of Mormon. At the same time I happened to see a social media post where someone posed the question, "What if you treated the Book of Mormon like your phone?" The video showed someone carrying the scriptures around, sharing something funny from it, reading it while on the train, walking, eating, etc. It was a great reminder. Within just a few days of that practice, I felt an increase of covenant power, subtle but significant.

Then one morning, I awoke and the anxiety was gone. Completely gone. My first thought was, Is this for real?

And then I thought, "Lord, how is it done?"

It still amazes me.

Let me say, for those dealing with anxiety clinically, genetically, or frequently, this is likely not a typical experience and I wouldn't want to suggest that. Counseling, medication, and consistent practices are all part of that healing equation.

---

67. Garrett H. Garff, "Spencer W. Kimball: Man of Action," *Ensign*, January, 2007, Gospel Library App.

I share only to express the wonder at the working of this principle. The increase of covenant power I felt was real and meaningful.

What is one way you have felt divine Covenant Comfort?

What is one way you want or need to feel that Christ-centered Covenant Comfort?

What is one thing you can do to make yourself open to or better able to receive that divine Covenant Comfort?

Christ-centered Covenant Capacity

For over 25 years I've been teaching women to find their purpose and then fulfill it, especially as an influential speaker, writer, and media presence for Him. But the odd thing was, generally when I experienced a certain kind of success, it seemed that Heavenly Father suddenly removed me from it. It was as if through many years of being a speaker, writer, and media presence, nothing seemed to really take off. In a way, it felt that He was intentionally plugging me in and out of the experiences but for reasons I couldn't see.

Have you felt that confusion before? That you know He has a plan but you can't see it?

Fast forward to a few years ago, I felt the rumble that I now needed to teach the women through retreats. I had never done such a thing, and though it doesn't sound too scary, it was entirely terrifying. Because this prompting came in September of 2020—in the thick of COVID.

Who in the world would create or register for a first-time, in-person retreat during COVID?

Exactly.

But I knew in my soul it was the right thing to do (Covenant Confidence). So I took the steps, did the hard things, and the Lord helped me fill that retreat ahead of schedule. (And we safely met together and no one got COVID). As I trained these women, there and afterward, I watched them learn, grow, and achieve in miraculous ways to share their purpose-driven messages to people they were meant to reach.

Suddenly, the Lord's plugging me in and out made sense. He didn't need me to do one thing and focus on me. He wanted to increase my capacity to teach others and to reach more people instead of moving forward by myself.

In that beautiful twofer way, He helped both myself and others experience successful growth because of it.

Christ-centered Covenant Capacity is like that. It's a limitless ability to flourish in your true divine self while doing that very same thing for those around you. It's not just having the confidence but the ability to do what He needs you to do, especially when you think you can't.

Though I've seen divine Covenant Capacity in many ways, here are two to consider.

1. Christ-centered Covenant Capacity to have the clarity and ability to do what you can't on your own.

Because He experienced Gethsemane, Golgotha, and the Garden Tomb, the Savior has perfect capacity to do and be all things, and He is eager to share that capacity with us. We get to plug into His energy source and use it to create, nurture, and flourish all that we wisely desire to do for good.

Elder Hales taught:

> The attributes of the Savior . . . develop in us in interactive ways. In other words, we cannot obtain one Christlike characteristic without also obtaining and influencing others. As one characteristic becomes strong, so do many more.[68]

His Covenant Capacity can be applied in seemingly temporal as well as spiritual ways. When my 18 year old was ready to move out, she was not, in fact, ready. Maybe you've experienced this too. Even though I'd had several young adult children move out, I wasn't sure how to respond. So I did a parental go-to, which was, set a deadline (translate: ultimatum). The ultimatum being that if she didn't have a job with x amount of hours by graduation then she would be choosing to work at home for me, for free.

After a week or so of this work-at-home torture, she put grease into the get-a-job problem and found a good possibility. I still remember

---

68. Robert D. Hales, *Becoming a Disciple of Our Lord Jesus Christ*, General Conference (Salt Lake City, UT), April, 2017. Gospel Library App.

her going to apply in person, working up the courage to do it, and calling me to get an extra boost.

But she did it. And in talking with the store manager found out one of her friends worked there too. One thing led to another and she was hired, and she had a successful summer.

Her capacity increased in the doing—in the faith-driven moments of her needing to face normal young adult fears. She did tedious research, asked difficult questions, held intimidating conversations, faced rejection, and was her bold self. And spiritually, she continued to pray, fast, keep her temple covenants, and involve the Lord. In short, she became. During that time, as a parent I also kept my temple covenants, seeking additional protection and guidance for her through my obedience to Him. Through this learning experience, she saw that keeping her covenants and doing all she could do increased her capacity for greater faith, energy, and ability to do the hard thing in the moment, as well as get great results. For her, it was a relief. For me, it was an incredible moment of watching a fast time-lapse experience of her growing before my eyes.

That's divine Covenant Capacity. It means using His covenant power to give you increased skills and understanding, this knowing in the moment what needs to be done, and then being able to actually do it, most especially when you don't think you can.

2. Covenant Capacity to handle emotional and mental difficulties.

For so many, especially young adults, our day feels like pulling four handcarts across the emotional plains. A Time magazine study on stress shared that out of the 45% of Gen Z individuals who responded, 91% of them said they had felt emotional stress symptoms such as depression or anxiety.[69]

My young adult daughter experienced this for herself. A few years ago, she left on her mission to France, sick as a dog, not sure she could make her entrance date. However, she rose, sick as a dog, and made it. Although she had hoped for wonderful companions and positive

---

69. Jamie Ducharme, "More Than 90% of Generation Z Is Stressed Out. And Gun Violence is Partly To Blame," *Time Magazine*, Oct. 30, 2018; htttps://time.com/5437646/gen-z-stress-report/

experiences, the mission experience was not what she had anticipated. Then COVID hit and she was one of the thousands of European missionaries who experienced lockdown along with a companion dealing with her own challenges. They could only go outside for one hour a day and had to have a legal paper confirming their right to do so.

During this extremely difficult time, she worked hard to stay on her mission and completed it a few months later. After returning home, she spent the next few years processing and recovering from the experience. I watched her wrestle with difficult periods of choosing to be faithful rather than complain and focus on how to move forward rather than stay stuck. She worked with the Lord to overcome perfectionism and recalibrate her daily expectations. She asked thoughtful questions, sought appropriate counseling, and used healthy spiritual and temporal practices to stay grounded, including breathing, yoga, journaling, and therapy.

Throughout the process, she had varying feelings about Heavenly Father and His love for her. She struggled with fallout from childhood experiences and behaviors of others that had created spiritual distortion. But amidst the uncertainty, she kept her covenants, kept trying to feel more of His spirit and love, and kept trying to clear out the emotional clutter.

Then she had a powerful experience.

Before the start of one summer she was focused on getting a new job. Loving travel, languages, cultures, and being of service, she wrote a specific list of her ideal job that included: just for summer, use French language skill, travel and lodging included, be paid to work, be in a beautiful environment.

Out of the blue, neighbors in a different ward who ran a travel agency in Europe offered her a job to work for the summer in Switzerland. And with that, every single item on her list was met. During that incredible summer, now called "The Switzerland Principle," she later shared that talking with Him on the long drives and in beautiful scenery, she felt His comfort and clarity every day. Though a few years before she had been down in the emotional valley, He had worked through covenant power to take her, literally, to the mountain top of the Alps.

I share this to show the contrast. In the first situation, my daughter kept her covenants and she had an extremely difficult experience with her mission in France. In the second situation, she kept her covenants and had an incredible life-changing experience in Switzerland. In both experiences, she was sustained, guided, and increased in her capacity to handle it by the Lord through that covenant power. He was able to let her know that He was not only there for her, but had always been, and would continue to be.

Ulisses Soares shares that:

> If we are steadfast and do not waver in our faith, the Lord will increase our capacity to raise ourselves above the challenges of life. We will be enabled to subdue negative impulses, and we will develop the capacity to overcome even what appear to be overwhelming obstacles.[70]

His Covenant Capacity is real and expansive. And as we pay attention, we can see and feel how Heavenly Father and the Savior are increasing our ability to deal with the challenges.

A Bonus Thought

Sometimes being able to see and feel that capacity can be difficult. One day, another adult daughter texted me and said, Mom, I really feel I need to do baptisms at the temple. Will you come with me? (When you get a request like that, you drop everything else.)

For a long time and due to childhood trauma, she had felt distanced from Heavenly Father and couldn't feel His love; that He wasn't seeing her or aware of her. She shared with me that on different occasions she was reminded specifically of the temple; was prompted to read her patriarchal blessing where temple was mentioned; and found the word "temple" in the scriptures.

Multiple tender mercies made this impromptu temple trip happen. My packed schedule was cleared; my young son was able to go to the neighbor's; and when we arrived we had only about a five-minute wait. And along the way, though there were very few people attending the temple at that moment, my daughter met three friends.

---

70. Ulisses Soares, *Confide in God Unwaveringly*, General Conference (Salt Lake City, UT), April 2017, Gospel Library App.

Afterward as we talked about the experience, she confessed she didn't feel very different and still wondered if He saw her. I was blown away. In that moment, I had the fabulous opportunity to point out the tender mercies that I had seen all day long. Sometimes, we just can't see the access to His Covenant Capacity increase, but it's most definitely there.

Experience It

What is one way you can see He has sustained you in a trial or challenge? What is one situation where He made you more capable than you had thought? What is one way you can open up to increasing your divine Covenant Capacity?

Wrapping Up

When we consider the innumerable gifts and blessings from His covenant power, it stuns me to consider that Heavenly Father and the Savior are so quick to share it with us. This divine covenant power really is that "super power" that makes our lives better, happier, and more fulfilling regardless of what the daily challenges may be. It's a power that buoys, sustains, and carries us through.

President Nelson shares this thought:

> [E]ntering into a covenant relationship with God binds us to Him in a way that makes everything about life easier. Please do not misunderstand me: I did not say that making covenants makes life easy. In fact, expect opposition, because the adversary does not want you to discover the power of Jesus Christ. But yoking yourself with the Savior means you have access to His strength and redeeming power.[71]

As we open our eyes to how covenant power shows up in our lives, we can see and access more Christ-centered Covenant Confidence, Covenant Comfort, and Covenant Capacity.

This is your hand-waving Jedi moment, an invitation to more fully choose the covenant path and increase your capacity to intentionally

---

71. Russell M. Nelson, *Overcome the World and Find Rest*, General Conference (Salt Lake City, UT), Oct 2022, Gospel Library App.

stay on it. Through covenant power, you can then experience the promised joy, peace, and fulfillment now, and in the eternities.

XVIII
The Price to Know Him
By Dru Huffaker

The Journey Begins

> The loads on the handcarts were greater than ever before, most carts having 100 pounds of flour on, besides ordinary baggage. The tents also were carried on the carts. The company was provisioned for sixty days, a daily ration of one pound of flour per head, with about half a pound for children, being the principal item.[72]

Years ago, my husband and I were asked to join a group of 500 youth and their leaders as they pulled handcarts for three days across Wyoming's rugged plains. We rode rickety old school buses for more than 400 miles to Martin's Cove, and a diverse mix of participants disembarked—some with eager anticipation, others dragged along by well-meaning leaders. Here, where weary travelers once forged a sacred path to Zion, we gathered to repeat part of their journey westward. We hoped to experience and come to understand what many of us

---

72. John Jaques, "Some Reminiscences," *Salt Lake Herald-Republican*, Dec. 29, 1878, 1.

had only heard from the pulpit and at Pioneer Day commemorations. Trek reenactments often focus on retelling the faith-filled, inspiring stories of the early Latter-day Saints, but ours also attempted to recreate some of the physical hardship and losses they endured. Heavy loads, intentionally simple meals, and long, hot hours on a dusty trail were expected.

Trouble on the Trail

> [The weather was] very cold. . . . You can imagine [between] five and six hundred Men, Women, & Children, worn down by drawing their hand carts through snow and mud; fainting by the way side; falling, chilled by the cold; children crying, from the cold their limbs stiffened by cold, their feet bleeding, and some of them bear to snow and frost. The sight is almost to much for the stoutest of us.[73]

The harsh landscape unfolded as we hauled over fifty handcarts loaded with tents, sleeping bags, water, and basic supplies. Dressed in newly sewn bonnets and petticoats, wide-brimmed hats and suspenders, we left the trailhead. The first day was hot and difficult, but we had fresh legs, and the youth especially had energy to spare. But on the brisk, cool morning of the second day, we baked our johnny cakes over an open fire and mentally prepared to face a daunting challenge. A strenuous route of about thirteen miles over Rocky Ridge rose before us in high peaks, reaching an elevation of 7,300 feet. The climb would transpire in the soon-to-be sweltering summer heat. Initially, spirits were high. Giggles and laughter filled the air at the outset, but brevity soon gave way to solemn silence as the magnitude of the undertaking became real.

Crumbling rock formations stood as silent sentinels and bore witness to the trials of those who had traversed this unforgiving terrain before us. Dirt constantly blew in our faces, kicked up from the handcarts traveling ahead, and it wasn't long before every person was covered with a layer of sweat and grit as well as hoards of eager ticks. We

---

73. George D. Grant to Brigham Young, November 2, 1856, Brigham Young Collection, Church Archives.

CHAPTER XVIII: THE PRICE TO KNOW HIM

pushed our heavy loads through streams of muddy water, with searing jolts stinging our newly blistered hands and ankles.

The discomfort was intense, but it seemed ungrateful to complain of temporary and elective hardships, especially when compared to the loss and suffering of the early Saints. I was also acutely aware that the eyes of the youth were observing us, their leaders, to see how we handled the strain. I tried to remain upbeat and encouraging in spite of my own exhaustion. The wheels creaked and groaned, echoing through the canyon walls, sounds that became familiar to us and were surely well known by travelers of the past. As we pushed forward, we retold stories of their courage, drawing strength from their legacy and developing a newfound appreciation for their sacrifices and fortitude.

JOY AND LOSS

> We buried our dead, got up our teams and about nine o'clock a.m. commenced ascending the Rocky Ridge. This was a severe day. The wind blew hard and cold. The ascent was some five miles long and some places steep and covered with deep snow. We became weary, set down to rest, and some became chilled and commenced to freeze.[74]

Along the way, participants were presented with a novel assignment: to care for ten-pound bags of flour as surrogate babies for the duration of the trip. These flour infants required constant attention, but they were joyously given old-fashioned family names and adorned with makeshift clothes crafted from bandanas. They were doted on, sung to, and played with, but the excitement was eventually tempered by the simple challenge of carrying the babies. As hours passed and traveling became increasingly arduous, the caretakers trudged along with their infants in their arms, struggling with the extra weight and responsibility.

Tragically and unexpectedly, as the day continued, men dressed in dark clothing approached the handcarts bearing a sober message as "angels of death." With solemnity, the men would drape a black cloth over some of the babies, declaring them dead. We were surprised to see

---

74. Stewart E. Glazier, ed., *Journal of the Trail* (Salt Lake City, UT: The Church of Jesus Christ of Latter-day Saints, 1996), 56.

how many of the young parents became emotional as they dug shallow graves using rocks and sticks and struggled to find the words to say goodbye. As I reflected on actual pioneer parents, I could scarcely imagine the anguish of watching their little ones experience extreme suffering and death. Yet they believed that braving these trials would fortify their families and draw them nearer to their Heavenly Father, in this world or the next, despite the immense sorrow and loss they faced.

Angels: Heavenly and Human

> I have looked back many times to see who was pushing my cart, but my eyes saw no one. I knew then that the angels of God were there.[75]

Gratefully, in contrast, as the day wore on, the landscape was also dotted with "angels" dressed in white. It lifted our hearts to see them, and we felt comforted knowing that they were watching over us. Their presence encouraged us, urging us onward as a reminder of the eternal rewards that come to those who endure.

While observing our company along the trail, I was surprised by some members of our group. I saw them selflessly carry fellow travelers to the other side of river crossings to keep them safe and dry, even though it meant that they themselves would be walking in wet, muddy clothing and be more prone to blisters. I saw them share food and gear in an attempt to bring each other comfort.

We did our best to support the youth, and we expected them to voice complaints, but as leaders, our greatest concern was for the silent ones. They were often the most likely to succumb to dehydration and sun exposure. In one instance, as we pushed side by side behind a cart, a petite young woman from our ward noiselessly toppled forward in a faint. Before I had time to process what had happened, one of our young men, a popular football player, had already rushed forward, scooped her into his arms, and taken off running to the medical support team. I was so impressed by the amount of consideration and awareness many of the young people had for the needs of those

---

75. William R. Palmer, "Francis Webster," *Instructor* 79 (May 1944): 217–18.

around them, and I couldn't help but think that they too were angels on the trail.

Enduring Well Together

> I began to draw the Handcart this morning but was obliged to leave it. Br. Francis Webster very kindly persuaded me to get on his handcart and drew me 17 miles. Elder Hunter and the two sisters Brown very kindly drew me about 4 miles. For which kindness I feel grateful, and pray God to bless them with health and strength.[76]

Amid the physical exertion and the blistering heat, we found ourselves drawing closer together. We sang to lighten our spirits and helped each other when the carts became stuck and impassable. We shared what we had in order to lift each other's burdens. As members of our company became injured or spent, they were lifted onto handcarts and carried. Unexpectedly, some who seemed most physically capable of completing the trek were exhausted and unable to continue. Men of all ages wept when the women were asked to pull the handcarts alone up one of the longest, steepest climbs. The men were instructed to stand by as the women struggled, watching helplessly as we fought our way up the mountain, stumbling over stones and mustering strength to keep the carts rolling forward. They knew how difficult it was to pull the carts, even with a fresh team of young men, and they were aware of how much we had depended on their strength. As I pushed alongside the other women, I considered earlier pioneer sisters traversing across the wilderness like this, for over a thousand miles and largely on their own, in what must surely have felt like an insurmountable feat.

Finally, with more than twelve hours of struggling behind us and feeling utterly exhausted, we reached the summit of Rocky Ridge. A quiet reverence settled over the group. For us, the journey was more than just an incredibly difficult physical feat—it was a connection to the past, a deepening of our faith, and a renewed commitment to our Savior. As we stood atop the ridge, gazing out at the vast Wyoming wilderness, we knew that while this physical endeavor was nearly

---

76. James G. Bleak, Journal, September 15, 1856, Church Archives.

complete, our spiritual pilgrimage would not come to an end. These were steps to a new beginning—a gradual process of discovery, gratitude, and growth, leading to a deeper understanding of our relationship with God.

We Too Are Not Forsaken

> We suffered beyond anything you can imagine and many died of exposure and starvation, but did you ever hear a survivor of that company utter a word of criticism? Not one of that company ever apostatized or left the Church, because every one of us came through with the absolute knowledge that God lives for we became acquainted with him in our extremities. . . . Was I sorry that I chose to come by handcart? No. Neither then nor any minute of my life since. The price we paid to become acquainted with God was a privilege to pay.[77]

As I have studied the lives of the early members of the restored Church, it has become clear to me that despite the difficulty, staggering loss, steady stream of tribulation, and their eventual pilgrimage to the Salt Lake Valley, the Saints were never left to carry their burdens alone. They faced each hardship with help, either from heaven or from mortal "angels" who lifted and lightened the weight of their distress, sometimes even at great personal sacrifice. The Lord was with them, strengthening and comforting them. Miracles, massive and minute, punctuated their journey. Yes, they suffered. No one can deny it. I imagine the Savior weeping with them, as He did for Lazarus, mourning with them as their hearts were breaking. I believe He also rejoiced with them as they sang and dreamt of Zion. And when they did not have the strength to continue, He either lifted their burden once more or welcomed them home with open arms.

We too are not spared difficulty in this life. Heartbreak, illness, personal struggle, and death are unfortunately a part of every mortal's experience to some degree. But in the quiet moments of my life, I am drawn to a profound truth: that seeking Jesus lies at the heart of our spiritual journey, despite (and because of) the heaviness of mortality. There is no greater calling, no nobler pursuit, than to intimately know

---

77. Palmer, "Francis Webster," 217–18.

Him, to testify of His divinity, and to try our best to become like Him. And miraculously, while we are on this journey, the greatest comfort we can receive is the knowledge that He is there and that He knows our hearts—that He loves us and will never leave us to face the bitter cup alone. As Doctrine and Covenants 84:88 states, "And whoso receiveth you, there I will be also, for I will go before your face. I will be on your right hand and on your left, and my Spirit shall be in your hearts, and mine angels round about you, to bear you up."

The reality is that each of us will be tested and refined in the fire of life. No one escapes unscathed. But although each of us will traverse our own path and face various obstacles, the Lord has promised to be with us. What does it mean to become acquainted with God in our extremities? Hardship and circumstance can weigh heavily upon us, but in quiet moments of internal anguish, we can turn to Him, feel His peace, and hear His voice. Like those early Saints who came before us, we must learn to trust in the promises of Jesus Christ and let that relationship lift and transform us. If in the end our heartache leads us to Him, it will all be worth it.

XIX
Fixing Our Focus on Jesus Christ

By John Hilton III

Has a question ever changed your life?

A woman named Janice sat in a church meeting reading Philippians 4:8, which says, "Whatsoever things are true, whatsoever things are honest, whatsoever things are just, whatsoever things are pure, whatsoever things are lovely, whatsoever things are of good report; if there be any virtue, and if there be any praise, think on these things."

As she pondered this verse, she felt the Holy Spirit ask her, "What about that show you love watching? Is there anything honest, pure, or lovely in it?"

Janice was shocked. She loved watching that show. But as she pondered the question, she had to confess that there was little in it that was lovely, of good report, or praiseworthy. She felt the Spirit whisper a second question: "So what are you going to do about it?"[78] These

---

78. Janice Carleton, "The Question That Changed My Life," The Word among Us, accessed Jan. 31, 2024, https://wau.org/resources/article/re_the_question_that_changed_my_life/.

questions changed Janice's life as she acted on them by giving up her show and filling her life with more uplifting things.

The Book of Mormon contains 543 questions, many of which can help us receive promptings from the Holy Ghost. One question that I've recently reflected on comes from Jacob, who said, "Why not speak of the atonement of Christ, and attain to a perfect knowledge of him?" (Jacob 4:12).

Think about that question for a moment. Why should we not do as President Russell M. Nelson has invited and "Learn all [we] can about Jesus Christ?"[79]

Learning all we can about Jesus Christ will deepen our love for Him. And the more we love Him, the more we will follow Him. Following Him is the way to peace as President Nelson taught, "Whatever questions or problems you have, the answer is always found in the life and teachings of Jesus Christ."[80]

I love this idea of focusing our studies specifically on Jesus Christ. My colleague Josh Sears once told me, "What if instead of talking about scripture study, we talked about Christ study?" As we read the scriptures, we should forget about checking a box and instead focus on what these chapters are teaching us about Jesus Christ.

Learning all we can about Jesus Christ will not necessarily be easy. Notice the descriptions President Nelson uses: "As we **invest time in learning** about the Savior and His atoning sacrifice, we are drawn to [Him]."[81] "As we **seek to be** disciples of Jesus Christ, our efforts to hear Him need to be ever more intentional. It **takes conscious and consistent effort** to fill our daily lives with His words, His teachings, His truths."[82] These descriptions—"invest time," "seek to be," and "conscious and consistent effort"—suggest that coming to know Christ is not coincidental on our part. Learning about Jesus Christ is

---

79. Russell M. Nelson, "Prophets, Leadership, and Divine Law" (Worldwide Devotional for Young Adults, Jan. 8, 2017), Gospel Library.
80. Russell M. Nelson, "The Answer Is Always Jesus Christ," *Liahona*, May 2023, 127.
81. Russell M. Nelson, "Drawing the Power of Jesus Christ into Our Lives," *Ensign*, May 2017, 40; emphasis added.
82. Russell M. Nelson, "Hear Him," *Ensign*, May 2020, 89.

Chapter XIX: Fixing Our Focus on Jesus Christ

an active pursuit, not a passive one. It is worth our best efforts to learn all we can about Jesus Christ.

The Topical Guide Invitation

One of my favorite ways to focus my scripture study on Jesus Christ has been to take President Nelson's invitation to study every verse about Jesus Christ in the Topical Guide. President Nelson gave this invitation to young adults in 2017.[83] He later explained that he had done this assignment himself, and that it changed his life. He recounted, "When I finished that exciting exercise, my wife asked me what impact it had on me. I told her, 'I am a different man!'"[84] He continued:

> For me, to be able to accomplish this assignment was just thrilling! . . . I have devoted much of my 92 years to learning about the Savior, but rare are the occasions when I have been able to learn as much as I did over this six-week study period.
>
> Now, I realize some of you are probably thinking to yourselves that you couldn't possibly have time to complete an assignment like this.
>
> I know how you feel. I thought the same thing of myself—that there's no way I can have time to do all of this. I needed to remind myself that . . . a faith-promoted comment would be "I know I don't have time for this, but I'm going to make time for it. And I'll fulfill it with what time I have."
>
> To those of you who feel you don't have time, if you will make a sacrifice, you will be well rewarded and very, very grateful for the change of perspective, increased knowledge, and improved depth of your conversion. I know this is true because I have seen the same rewards in my own life. . . .
>
> I promise you that if you will study His words, your ability to be more like Him will increase. I know this is true."[85]

I discovered for myself that President Nelson's promises are true. In the fall of 2017, I moved to Jerusalem and decided that, since there

---

83. Russell M. Nelson, "Prophets, Leadership, and Divine Law," 39.
84. Russell M. Nelson, "Drawing the Power of Jesus Christ into Our Lives."
85. Russell M. Nelson, "Study the Savior's Words," *Ensign*, Jan. 2018.

were no nearby temples, I would dedicate my normal temple time to completing President Nelson's invitation. Each week I went to the Garden of Gethsemane, the Garden Tomb, or the Church of the Holy Sepulcher and spent some time reading the verses about Jesus Christ that were listed in the Topical Guide.

I especially enjoyed reading about specific aspects of Jesus Christ in a concentrated form. For example, looking up "Jesus Christ, Advocate" helped me see repeated references to the Savior's advocacy. Seeing multiple verses all in a row helped this aspect of the Savior's nature sink a little deeper into my heart. The same was true for many other entries. I didn't study all 2,200 verses in six weeks like President Nelson did; it took me closer to nine months. But at the end I felt like I received the blessings President Nelson promised—specifically a deeper testimony of and connection to Jesus Christ.

Study the Book of Mormon

Of course, studying every Topical Guide verse about Jesus Christ is not the only way to learn all we can about him. In 2021, Elder David A. Bednar gave the following idea for growing closer to Christ through scripture study. He said, "My invitation . . . is, go into the Book of Mormon. Read it from the beginning to the end, looking for the Savior—His attributes, His characteristics. And as you do that, earnestly and sincerely, it no longer becomes looking at words on a page. You come to hear His voice. You come to know Him in a very remarkable way."[86]

Many of us have had the experience of reading the Book of Mormon and looking for every reference to Jesus Christ. I recently did this, but instead of only looking for the names of Jesus Christ, I also looked for pronouns that refer to Him. Consider Alma 33:22: "Begin to believe in **the Son of God**, that **he** will come to redeem **his** people, and that **he** shall suffer and die to atone for their sins; and that **he** shall rise again from the dead, which shall bring to pass the resurrection, that all men shall stand before **him**, to be judged at the last and judgment day" (emphasis added).

---

86. "Face to Face with Elder and Sister Bednar: Ask, Seek, Knock" (worldwide broadcast for young adults, Sept. 12, 2021), Gospel Library.

If we were only looking for names, we would find only one in this verse. However, the Savior is mentioned five additional times. This verse emphasizes that Jesus Christ is not only the Son of God, but He is also the one to redeem us through his everlasting Atonement and Resurrection, and He will be our judge. When I looked for pronouns referring to Jesus Christ, the number of total references that I found concerning Jesus Christ nearly doubled. That gives us twice as many Book of Mormon references to explore, to learn more about the character, nature, and teachings of Jesus Christ.

Memorize and Focus on His Words

In 2 Nephi 32:3, Nephi says, "Feast upon the words of Christ; for behold, the words of Christ will tell you all things what ye should do." I always read this as a reference to scripture in general, but what if we thought about feasting specifically on the words of Christ? What would this look like?

I recently read the Book of Mormon looking specifically for the words that Christ, Himself, spoke. As I did so, I noticed several details that I would have otherwise missed. Jesus Christ focuses on His *Father*, He emphasizes His *name*, and He frequently discusses the importance of being *baptized*. As I paid attention to the specific words of Jesus Christ, I learned more about what is important to Him—and as a result, those things became more important to me.

In addition, we can follow Elder Neil L. Andersen's counsel to memorize some of Christ's teachings. Speaking to missionaries in 2022, Elder Andersen taught, "I think it is very helpful if you begin today to learn a few of the teachings of Jesus Christ and have them in your memory . . . choose your own [passages to memorize]—find some things that Jesus has said and let them penetrate who you are."[87]

---

87. Scott Taylor, "Elder Andersen shares lists of scriptures, parables and testimonies — and asks missionaries to create their own," *Church News*, Mar. 9, 2022, https://www.thechurchnews.com/2022/3/9/23216857/elder-andersen-mtc-shares-lists-scriptures-parables-testimonies-asks-missionaries-to-create-own.

Watching Movies

At this point, some of you might be thinking, "This sounds like a lot. Read 2,000 verses from the Topical Guide, carefully study the Book of Mormon, memorize scriptures . . . couldn't I just watch a movie?"

Of course!

My first memory of watching a movie about Jesus was as a nineteen-year-old in the Provo Missionary Training Center. A large group of missionaries gathered to watch a Church video, *The Lamb of God*. As I saw the Savior nailed to the cross, the Spirit washed over me and testified to me that what I was seeing really happened. Movies can be a powerful vehicle for feeling the Holy Ghost. Some people are concerned that movies might inaccurately depict certain scenes from the Savior's life, but I believe this doesn't need to detract from the many things we can learn and feel from artistic media. Instead, as my colleague Matt Grey shared, movies can be a catalyst for learning about the Savior. He said:

> For me, placing Jesus films, the New Testament text, and historical sources into thoughtful conversation has prompted valuable questions that I might not otherwise have asked about a wide range of issues, including Jesus's appearance, personality, teachings, and ongoing social relevance, as well as the nature of scriptural writings. Often these questions come as I find myself wondering why film directors made certain decisions, how I might have presented things differently as a believing historian, and what the implications of those decisions might be for the spiritual experience of the viewers. I often find that asking those type of questions facilitates richer inspiration as a teacher, academic insights as a scholar, and spiritual experiences as a believer, all of which have been a great blessing in my personal efforts to get to know Jesus better.[88]

If you're interested in doing a little study activity with scriptural scenes from movies, visit https://johnhiltoniii.com/thechosen/. On this page, you'll find links to short clips from *The Chosen* based on the

---

88. Scott C. Esplin and Matthew J. Grey, "From Scripture to Screen: Films Depicting Jesus and the World of the New Testament," *Winter 2021 Review Magazine*, https://rsc.byu.edu/winter-2021/scripture-screen.

scripture passages they connect with. Try watching some of these clips and reading the scriptural passages that are connected with them.

Artwork

Art scholar Noel A. Carmack wrote that "the motivating impact that visual images of Christ have on members of The Church of Jesus Christ of Latter-day Saints cannot be overestimated."[89] Many Latter-day Saints have reported that seeing an image of the Savior has influenced them in positive ways. For example, one individual told me, "I recently created a folder of images of Jesus that rotate through the lock screen on my phone. Seeing a different image of Christ each time I unlock my phone keeps it new and interesting and reminds me to center my thoughts on the Savior." A young man described how a painting of Christ in his room affected his behavior: "When I awake in the morning, I look at that picture. Because of my testimony of the Savior, I consciously make a decision to honor his name during the day."[90]

In May 2020, the First Presidency sent a letter directing that "framed artwork that focuses on the Savior should always be displayed" in "meetinghouse entries and foyers," specifically "artwork that depicts the Savior Himself or the Savior ministering to others."[91] Although I'm not aware of such an injunction being given regarding artwork in our homes, Christ-centered artwork could certainly invite the Spirit. I recently talked with a college student who was struggling with pornography. "In order to strengthen myself spiritually," she told me, "I've put up some images of Jesus Christ in my dorm room. That helps me stay focused on Him."

President Spencer W. Kimball would often tell the story of a mother who sorrowed because each of her sons went off to sea after high school rather than serving a full-time mission. "The mother tearfully

---

89. Noel A. Carmack, "Images of Christ in Latter-day Saint Visual Culture, 1900–1999," *BYU Studies Quarterly* 39, no. 3 (2000): 19.
90. Ronan Head, "Picture Perfect," *New Era*, May 1995, 14–15, cited in Carmack, "Images of Christ in Latter-day Saint Visual Culture," 19.
91. "Art in Meetinghouse Foyers and Entryways to Reflect a Deeper Reverence for Jesus Christ," *Church Newsroom*, May 11, 2020, https://newsroom.churchofjesuschrist.org/article/art-foyers-entryways-reverence-jesus-christ.

asked her bishop why he thought it was so when she had hoped her sons would further their education and accept mission calls. The bishop had no answer—until one day when he visited her home and saw framed on the wall a painting of a ship at sea. With sudden understanding the bishop said, 'Now I understand. You have been an excellent teacher. Every day of their lives you have taught your sons the romance and adventure of the sea. No wonder they all wanted to join the Navy.'"[92]

While there is certainly nothing wrong with an image of a ship at sea, this experience invites us to consider the impact of the visual images we choose to display. One mother told me of her strategy for helping her children have artwork of Jesus Christ in their bedrooms: "I took them to a Christian bookstore," she said, "and asked them which picture of Jesus they liked best. Later I went back and purchased that image, framed it, and gave it to them for Christmas." Do we already have Christ-centered artwork prominently displayed in our homes? If not, how might doing so influence us and those we love?

Conclusion

Other ideas—such as learning from modern prophets, listening to Christ-centered music, or reading academic books—could be added to our list. If you're interested in more ideas for fixing your focus on Jesus Christ, I've listed more than twenty on my website.[93]

The more we learn about Jesus Christ, the more we deeply feel and know that it really will all be worth it. Jacob's question "Why not speak of the atonement of Christ, and attain to a perfect knowledge of him?" (Jacob 4:12) has changed my life. Focusing on Jesus Christ will help each of us know Him better, love Him more, and feel a greater desire to keep His commandments. Let us all take President Nelson's invitation: "Learn all you can about Jesus Christ."[94]

---

92. "The Temple Photograph Series," *Ensign*, Apr. 1977, 96.
93. See https://johnhiltoniii.com/learn-of-me/.
94. Russell M. Nelson, "Prophets, Leadership, and Divine Law."

About the Authors

Julie Lee

Julie Lee's personal experiences with human connection saved her life and changed the trajectory of her career.

As a keynote speaker, Julie shows leaders exactly how to saturate their work culture with human connection to improve the mental health of their people so they can perform at peak potential. Recognized for her ingenuity and passion, Julie Lee is the head speaking coach for The Relevant Speaker, a one-of-its-kind program that helps aspiring speakers build a profitable speaking business.

Julie Lee is the author of *I See You: How Compassion and Connection Save Lives* and the children's book *Broccolipunzle: A Girl with Extraordinary Hair*. Her podcast, *I See You*, has inspired thousands of listeners to succeed in relationships by embracing human connection. Fueled by her genuine nature to help others thrive, Julie currently cohosts the podcast *Love, ADHD*. She enjoys living by the mountains in Utah with her two children, Samuel and Lydia.

Learn more about Julie's work at julieleespeaks.com.

Reyna Aburto

Reyna Aburto was born in Nicaragua and is married to Carlos Aburto from Mexico. They live in Orem, Utah, and have three children and three grandchildren.

Reyna studied industrial engineering in Nicaragua and holds a degree in computer science from Utah Valley University. She has worked in the language industry for more than thirty years and owns a translation business with her husband. She has served as the Second Counselor in the General Relief Society Presidency, as a member of the Primary General Board, and in various callings in the Church. She currently serves on the Correlation Materials Evaluation Committee in Church Headquarters.

Reyna is a member of several governing boards. She is the author of *Reaching for the Savior* (*Acudamos al Salvador* in Spanish) and the cohost of the *Consecrating Your Life* podcast (@consecratingpod) with her daughter Elena.

Michelle Craig

Michelle Craig finds great joy in being a wife, mother of three, and nana to twelve. She is a disciple of Jesus Christ and recently completed her service as First Counselor in the Young Women General Presidency. During her service, she was blessed to meet many around the world who follow the example of Jesus Christ and "go about doing good." She has great hope for the rising generation and their capacity to make a difference in the world.

Lori Denning

Lori L. Denning is a scholar and scripture enthusiast, pursuing her PhD in ancient scripture at Claremont Graduate University with a master's degree in theology from Gonzaga University. As a dedicated nerd, Lori even sings biblical Hebrew for fun. She has written three books, including the *Real Heroes Series*, and teaches at BYU. Lori also appears as a frequent podcast guest and hosts the video series *The Bible Brief*. She served a mission in Barcelona, Spain.

A native of San Diego, Lori's adventurous spirit is seen in her love for dirt bikes, karaoke, and chocolate. With an identical twin (the cute one, she claims), her vibrant personality and diverse interests shine in everything she does.

Marianna Richardson

Marianna Richardson and her husband, Steve, have twelve children and thirty-two grandchildren. They served a mission together in São Paulo, Brazil. Her hobbies are keeping up with her family, traveling with her husband, and always learning. She currently teaches as an adjunct professor at the Marriott School of Business and serves as the director of communications for the G20 Interfaith Forum. She received both her MBA and JD degrees from BYU.

Portia Louder

Portia Louder spent four and a half years in prison and invites us to see the world from a different perspective. Portia is a writer, speaker, photographer, and advocate. She works with at-risk youth and women struggling with addiction. Portia authored a book titled *Living Louder: A Compassionate Journey through Federal Prison* in which she describes her most difficult experiences with deep affection. How do you fight despair and learn to meet the world with a loving heart? Portia teaches us those lessons, discovered in federal prison.

Learn more about Portia's experiences at portialouder.com.

MICHELLE WILSON

MICHELLE WILSON IS A WIFE, MOM, SPEAKER, and author of inspirational nonfiction, children's literature, and women's fiction. On the inspirational front, Michelle speaks and writes to women and young women, striving to help them access confidence, peace, and joy as they strengthen themselves and their relationships with God and others.

Michelle teaches gospel truths and empowering life principles with love and humor. She knows what it's like to be weighed down by guilt, shame, comparison, and self-doubt. She also knows how to be freed from those burdens and finds joy in sharing what she's learned with others. She loves laughter, sisterhood, family, optimism, and, most of all, her Father in Heaven and her Savior, Jesus Christ.

Visit michellewilsonwrites.com to discover more content from Michelle.

ELAINE S. DALTON

ELAINE S. DALTON WAS BORN AND RAISED in Ogden, Utah, and received her bachelor's degree in English from Brigham Young University. She served as the Young Women General President from 2008 until 2013, a calling that she feels was a grand privilege and blessing in her life. She also served as the chair of the board of trustees at Utah Valley University and is currently the president of the Stella Oaks Foundation. Her most important titles, however, are wife and best friend of Stephen Dalton, mother to six magnificent adult children, and grandmother. After fifty years of marriage, she and her husband now find themselves surrounded by twenty-one blonde-haired grandchildren!

Elaine enjoys being outdoors, hiking with her family, and dancing with her granddaughters. She has run seventeen marathons and completed two Boston Marathons. She is the author of three books for women and young women and speaks to groups of young women and women about their identity, potential, and purpose.

Elaine loves life and believes in people. She has great confidence in the rising generation of noble youth and often says, "I believe that one virtuous young woman or young man can change the world!"

Kimberly DowDell

Kimberly DowDell, married to her high school sweetheart for twenty-three years, is the proud mother of four wonderful children. After the birth of her fourth child, who was diagnosed with Down syndrome, Kimberly grappled with fears and anxieties, mourning the expectations she had held. This emotional turmoil led to depression and a profound sense of isolation. More than ever before, she discovered solace and renewed strength within her testimony of Jesus Christ and His Atonement. As she followed the promptings of the Spirit, she found the support and joy she desperately needed during this challenging time.

Today, via her Instagram page (@thekimberlydowdell), she openly shares the heartwarming and joyous moments of raising a child with Down syndrome. After her son's birth, she yearned for a glimpse into his future and found inspiration from a young man with Down syndrome on YouTube who ignited hope within her. Now she's paying it forward by providing others who receive a similar diagnosis a glimpse of the happiness and opportunities that await them through their own unique life journey.

Follow Kimberly on Instagram (@thekimberlydowdell), TikTok (@Kimberly.dowdell), or YouTube (@kimdancefitness143).

William Perez

Born and raised in Miami, Florida, William Perez is a PhD candidate in American religious history at Florida State University and a coordinator for seminaries and institutes in Tallahassee, Florida. He loves saltwater fish tanks and pizza movie nights with his wife, Tori, and their five daughters. William served in the Texas McAllen Mission and is fluent in Spanish. He has published work in Latter-day Saint theology and history as well as Afro-Caribbean religious traditions. He also enjoys leading tours to Israel and to Church history sites in the US as well as sharing gospel content on his YouTube channel, Latter-day Divers.

Fiona Smith

Fiona Smith has over a decade's worth of experience in TV, film, theater, research, and literature on nineteenth and twentieth century pioneers in Great Britain and the United States.

In England, Fiona earned a Bachelor of Laws (LLB) degree with honors and assisted in writing a documentary on the disparity in the criminal justice system for those with intellectual disabilities. In Utah, she graduated with a master's degree in theatre and media arts from Brigham Young University. Her thesis focused on early black American pioneers, including her role as Jane Manning James in the *Joseph Smith: Prophet of the Restoration* movie.

Fiona was the TV host for *Road to Zion*, a documentary on early pioneers. She also worked as a producer, TV manager, and writer for *Living Essentials*, a BYUtv live talk show on important how-to tips and tools for living. As a singer, Fiona has a cameo in *The Singles Ward* movie and sang alto in The Tabernacle Choir at Temple Square.

Fiona's creative pursuits include various forms of media that focus on projects bringing unique stories out of obscurity. She enjoys travel, art, photography, and writing choral music. Fiona also enjoys communicating in British Sign Language and German.

Boyd Matheson

Boyd Matheson is the host of KSL NewsRadio's *Inside Sources* and KSL TV's *Sunday Edition* and is a nationally recognized social and political commentator. Prior to joining KSL, he served as opinion editor for Deseret News, chief of staff in the United States Senate, and president of a public policy think tank and has spent years as an international business strategist. Boyd and his wife, Debbie, have five children and eight grandchildren, and he is currently serving for a season as disciple-bishop of the Manila 9th Ward.

Al Carraway

Al Carraway is a convert to the Church of Jesus Christ, award-winning international speaker, and multi-award winning and #1 best-selling author to more than eight published titles, including *Finding Yourself in the New Testament, My Dear Little One, More than the Tattooed Mormon, Walking with Joseph,* and *Wildly Optimistic!* Al has a deep love for guiding Church history tours twice a year as well as seminars at sea.

Since 2010, she has inspired others with her conversion and faith through difficult times. Her passion is to tell everyone that happiness exists and that it comes from Jesus—that He's real and tangible. She shares how to find and love Him in the hard, in the unwanted, and in the unexpected. Because through it all, with Him, we have every reason to be wildly optimistic.

Originally from New York, Al is now living in Charleston, South Carolina, with her husband, Benjamin, and her three kids.

Learn more about Al's books at alcarraway.com.

Michelle Porcelli

Michelle Porcelli is an elementary school counselor, corporate trainer, and TEDx speaker. She has written and instructed courses for BYU Independent Study and is an author with Cedar Fort Publishing & Media. She has also been a presenter for EFY and BYU Education Week. She graduated from Brigham Young University in 1993 and earned her master's degree in school counseling in 2011. She currently serves as stake Relief Society president where she has learned that service and initiative are the heart of the gospel.

She runs Hope Squads for two elementary schools and adores this age group. She believes that the world would be a much kinder place if we would follow the examples of little children, showing compassion, forgiveness, and unconditional love.

Michelle spends time spoiling her grandchildren, Max and Ivy. She thinks her five children and one daughter-in-law are the best people in the world. However, she knows her husband wins the trophy for most supportive and tolerant. She loves chocolate chip cookies and homemade bread and lives by the motto "Chins up—smiles on!"

Learn more about Michelle's work at michelleporcelli.com.

Tom Ballard

Tom Ballard is "The Heart Rock Guy." He is a kindness specialist, motivational speaker, and stone carver. His way of being kind? Making and distributing hundreds of thousands of heart rocks. He believes that people can use heart rocks to strengthen family ties, deepen friendships, and save lives.

Tom is a dynamic storyteller and loves sharing experiences he's had making and distributing heart rocks. As someone living with mental illness (bipolar disorder), Tom believes that using creativity and kindness is how we lift ourselves and others out of the darkness and struggles that we all experience. His goal is to distribute one million heart rocks by 2029.

Learn more about Tom's work and mission at takeheart.rocks.

Ganel-Lyn Condie

Ganel-Lyn Condie is a popular motivational speaker and author. As a graduate from Arizona State University, with a BS in elementary education and psychology, she became an award-winning journalist and editor of *Wasatch Woman* magazine. Ganel-Lyn is a regular television, podcast, and radio guest. Her talks, books, and media have now encouraged people all over the world. Ganel-Lyn's faith and family have helped her learn from all of life's stewardships.

Learn more about Ganel-Lyn's work at ganellyn.com.

Connie Sokol

Connie Sokol is a national speaker, best-selling author, TV and podcast personality, and mother of seven. She is a regular contributor on Studio 5 with Brooke Walker and the podcast host of *Called to Create*.

Connie is the founder of Disciple Thought Leaders, and through leadership retreats, she teaches women to find their purpose and fulfill it as influential speakers, writers, and a media presence for the Lord. She is also vice president of the National Speakers Association for the Mountain West Chapter. She enjoys spending time with her family and eating decadent treats.

Visit conniesokol.com to learn more about Connie's retreats, leadership circle, podcasts, and more.

Dru Huffaker

Dru Huffaker is a convert to The Church of Jesus Christ of Latter-day Saints and is passionate about her love of Jesus Christ and the restored gospel. She is married to her best friend, Mel, is the mother of six beautiful children, and is known as "Honey" to her seventeen grandchildren. She is the executive vice president of sales and marketing at Cedar Fort Publishing, the largest independent Latter-day Saint publisher. One of her greatest joys is teaching institute at BYU to a large all-freshman class of eager young adults preparing to serve missions. She is an avid family history buff and musical theater fan, can often be found cheering loudly at BYU games of all varieties, and loves spending time with her family and close friends.

John Hilton III

John Hilton III is a professor of religious education at Brigham Young University. John and his wife, Lani, have six children. They have lived in Boise, Boston, Miami, Mexico, Jerusalem, and China. John has a master's degree from Harvard and a PhD from BYU, both in education.

John has published several books, including *Considering the Cross* and *Voices in the Book of Mormon*. He is also the author of *The Book of Mormon: A Master Class*. John loves teaching, reading, spending time with his family, doing humanitarian work, snowboarding, and practicing magic tricks.

Discover more of John's content at johnhiltoniii.com.

About the Editors

Liz Kazandzhy

Liz Kazandzhy (kah-zahn-JEE) has worked as a professional book reviewer and top-rated editor, specializing in nonfiction genres such as self-help and religion. But as much as she loves reviewing and editing books, her real passion is writing them. Her books focus on presenting gospel doctrine in a way that's easy to understand and applicable to real life, and they include *The Holy Ghost from A to Z: What the Spirit Can Do for You*, *The Holy Ghost from A to Z for Kids*, and *Ask, Seek, Find: 1,000 Questions to Deepen Your Scripture Study*.

Liz served in the Ukraine Kyiv Mission, after which she graduated from BYU with a degree in human development. She and her husband, Vlad, currently live in Utah with their three daughters.

Learn more about Liz's books at lizkauthor.com.

Kyle Lund

Kyle Lund was raised in the redwoods of Humboldt County, California. He graduated with a bachelors degree in English literature and double minored in creative writing and politics from Souther Virginia University. When he isn't watching soccer matches, he can be found writing novels, reading, or spending time with his wife and son.